MARTIN HEIDEGGER

Logic as the Question Concerning
the Essence of Language

SUNY series in Contemporary Continental Philosophy
Dennis J. Schmidt, editor

Martin Heidegger

Logic as the Question Concerning the Essence of Language

Translated by
Wanda Torres Gregory and Yvonne Unna

Published by State University of New York Press, Albany

For information, contact State University of New York Press, Albany, NY
www.sunypress.edu

Production by Kelli W. LeRoux
Marketing by Anne M. Valentine

Library of Congress Cataloging-in-Publication Data
Heidegger, Martin, 1889-1976.
[Logik als die Frage nach dem Wesen der Sprache. English]
Logic as the question concerning the essence of language / Martin Heidegger ; translated by Wanda Torres Gregory and Yvonne Unna.
    p. cm. — (SUNY series in contemporary continental philosophy)
Includes bibliographical references.
ISBN 978-1-4384-2673-0 (hardcover : alk. paper)
ISBN 978-1-4384-2674-7 (pbk. : alk. paper)
1. Logic. 2. Language and languages—Philosophy. 3. Philosophical anthropology. 4. History—Philosophy. I. Title.
B3279.H48L62813 2009
160—dc22   2009006212

10 9 8 7 6 5 4 3 2

Published in German as *Logik als die Frage nach dem Wesen der Sprache*
© 1998 by Vittorio Klostermann. Frankfurt am Main.

GA II, 38. Freiburg lecture, summer semester 1934, on the basis of Wilhelm Hallwachs' transcript of the lecture. Edited by Günter Seubold.

The translation of this work was supported by a grant from the Goethe-Institut, which is funded by the German Ministry of Foreign Affairs.

CONTENTS

First Part
The Question Concerning the Essence of Language as
Fundamental and Guiding Question of All Logic

Second Part
The Original Time as the Ground of All Questions Hitherto and the
Resumption of the Question-Sequence in Reversed Direction

Translators' Foreword

This book is a translation of Martin Heidegger's lecture during the summer semester of 1934 at the University of Freiburg. The German text was published in 1998 as volume 38 of Heidegger's *Gesamtausgabe* (Collected Edition). It is based on transcripts by students who attended the lecture. Heidegger's lecture notes for the lecture were considered lost at the time of the publication of the German text. However, in 2006, these lecture notes were allegedly found in the estate of Elisabeth Baumgartner.[1] To our knowledge, there have been no public announcements since then on whether, when, and where these documents will be published.

Offered shortly after Heidegger's resignation as Rector of the University of Freiburg, the lecture provides new insights into his personal involvement with the National Socialist regime and into the political dimensions of his philosophy. Two of Heidegger's autobiographical remarks also give a clear sense of the special significance of the lecture in the development of his thoughts on language and logic:

> …it was all of twenty years after my doctoral dissertation that I dared discuss in a class the question of language.…In the summer semester of 1934, I offered a lecture series under the title "Logic." In fact, however, it was a reflection on the *logos*, in which I was trying to find the nature of language.[2]

Some people get stirred up because, after the reference in my inaugural address "What is Metaphysics?" (1929), I keep on raising the question of logic…[Since] my lectures "Logic," given in the summer of 1934, this title "Logic" conceals "the transformation of logic into the question of the essential nature of language"—a question that is something else again than the philosophy of language.[3]

Translating Heidegger is always a challenging feat, especially because of his abundant use of technical terms and neologisms. An understanding of key words and their interrelations often requires close attention to their etymologies. Moreover, when the roots of German and English words do not coincide, important nuances threaten to become invisible or incomprehensible in translation. We offer two forms of assistance to the English reader: a lexicon and additions to the text enclosed in brackets. The lexicon provides English translations only of those German terms that we believe are critical in the original text. We have inserted brackets in the text to signal important etymological relations at play, to distinguish between the German *Sein* and *Seiendes* when their English translation ("being") is ambiguous, to render a smoother translation, and to note problems in reading the original. The German terms *Dasein, Führer, Gleichschaltung, Reich, das Volk* (and its plural form: *Völker*), and *Weltanschauung* (and its plural form: *Weltanschauungen*) remain without translation because their respective English translations into "existence," "leader," "coordination," "empire," "the people," and "world-view," do not preserve their unique philosophical, cultural, or historical connotations.

We wish to thank our anonymous reviewer for the careful examination of the manuscript and sensitivity to the challenges of translating Heidegger. We are also grateful to Jane Bunker, Editor-in-Chief of SUNY Press, and to Dennis J. Schmidt, Editor of the SUNY Series in Contemporary Continental Philosophy, for their continued support of our translation projects. Finally, we would like to express our gratitude to the Torres Gregory family, David Walters, and Liam Unna Walters.

INTRODUCTION
Structure, Origin, Meaning and Necessary Shaking Up of Logic

The title "logic" is the abbreviation of the Greek expression "λογική." This expression means: concerning the λόγος. One should add: "ἐπιστήμη." ἐπιστήμη λογική is the knowledge that concerns the λόγος. Logic, as ἐπιστήμη λογική, means the knowing well of the λόγος. Yet, "λόγος" in general means saying and talking, that is, saying and talking in a particular meaning, conceived in a distinctive sense, namely as λόγος ἀποφαντικός. This is that saying that has in itself the performance and the tendency of showing, of pointing out. In the λόγος that shows and points out lies the essence of the proposition. The proposition is a particular kind of talking—in distinction from talk in the sense of commanding, demanding, asking, praising, proposing, scolding.

The propositional λόγος says how a thing is and what the matter is. Logic deals, therefore, with this asserting. Such asserting is pronounced, is pronounced to and is repeated by others. Pronounced propositions are put down in statements. These can also be written down and be preserved in literature. The λόγος is, hence, something that is in a certain sense always, like trees, mountains, forests, etc., that is present-at-hand, extant.

Propositions can be thus grasped in view in an immediate run-up, can be conceived in the examination. One can say how such a proposition looks as proposition. In such determination, a determinate knowledge of the proposition arises, the discovery of the right execution of the same and a being familiar within, for example, in talk and reply: in the dispute, to remain a match for the other in the manner of saying.

At first, we leave out of account here the different impulses. We are considering at first only the general manner in which logic was in the beginning immediately grasped in view, so to speak.

The reflection on the λόγος settled in at the end of the era of the great philosophy with Plato and Aristotle. Four respects were leading for this first knowledge of the λόγος; the λόγος was investigated under four different methods.

§ 1. The inner structure of logic

We are attempting now in advance to display briefly the general frame of the inner structure of logic under the four methods that determine the structure of logic since the Greeks up to us.

a) Analysis

The proposition is at first taken as something present-at-hand, like an extant thing. It encounters us at first in a pronounced statement, for example: "The sky is overcast." The statement as word-construction can be analyzed into the individual words "sky," "overcast," "is" – words to which particular representations correspond.

b) Assembly

"The sky is overcast" is nothing other than an interlacing (συμπλοκή), as the Greeks say. The proposition composed in this manner can now, in its turn, provide the piece from which a further structure of a logical kind is composed; for out of several statements a further logical construction can be assembled, that is, out of two judgments a third can be derived. The derivation of a third judgment out of two given ones consists in the combination of the concepts that are still not connected in these. This combination is only possible then, if it is mediated through a concept that is connected to both judgments.

> "All human beings are mortal."
> "Socrates is a human being."
> "Socrates is mortal."

We call such a collection of propositions a syllogism. In this assembly, one thus rises from the concept over the judgment (the proposition) to the conclusion.

c) Regulation

The third kind of consideration of these structures is regulation. Structures like judgments and syllogisms are at first ascertainable, present-at-hand. They have, however, a peculiar kind of being, different from things like stones and so on. Such propositions and statements are only insofar as they are constructed through the free activity of the human being. This construction, however, is not arbitrary, but subordinate to rules.

α) *The self-sameness of what is represented*

Every structure is subordinate to a particular fundamental rule. A concept that means a certain representation of something in general, for example, of sky, can only then be used as a fundamental piece of a proposition, if the content of the representation or the meaning of the word is thereby captured in its respective self-sameness; if we perhaps not unawares say "sky" and mean *tree*. We call this fundamental rule the fundamental rule of the self-sameness of what is represented.

β) *Non-contradiction*

For proposition or judgment the fundamental rule holds, which states: A concept can only then be assigned to another in the proposition, insofar as it does not contradict [the other]; and this concept must be denied of it, insofar as it contradicts [the other]. "A is B" and "A not non-B" cannot be true at the same time (valid until Hegel). This is the fundamental rule of non-contradiction.

γ) *The ordering of reason and consequence*

In the syllogism, the propositions are not lined up one after another at will, but the connection is determined and regulated by the ordering of reason and consequence.

Summed up we have, therefore:
— Principle of identity
— Principle of non-contradiction
— Principle of reason

With this, we have circumscribed the main elements of the province of logic (of the knowing of the λόγος).

d) Form consideration

We start from the fundamental phenomenon of logic, the proposition like, for example: "The sky is overcast." Corresponding to this proposition, we can construct another at will, for example: "The tree is blooming." Logic does not investigate these individual statements according to that which is said in them, but attends to something else. Though every proposition has a particular object, it is not the object that occupies logic, not whether it is or is not. At the same time, we already see from the kind of statements like, for example, "The sky is overcast" and "The number is odd," regardless of difference in factual content, a certain self-sameness in the manner in which objectification, accentuation, arranging, and determination take place, in each case according to the kind of fact of the area of being

We call this correspondence "form." Logic investigates the form, but not the material content. Therefore, the fundamental forms can be presented in signs like $A = B$, whereby A is arbitrary. Though every proposition has its object, for logic, the kind of object is arbitrary. Logic looks only at the forms of the proposition, it considers the forms of the fundamental structures and fundamental rules of asserting, and insofar as this consideration is organized and partitioned, logic becomes a science. It is the science of the *forms of the fundamental structures and fundamental rules of the proposition*.

§ 2. Logic as preparatory school for all thinking.
Grammar and logic. Logic history

Asserting encounters us commonly in language. The first reflection on the proposition has directed itself alongside language. Language came to be the leading thread of reflection on the proposition. That is why the doctrine of language also came to be in a peculiar relation to logic. Both determine themselves mutually. Logic determines grammar, and grammar determines logic, up to the present day—a peculiar interrelation that will still occupy us later. To contrast from the start the mere consideration of word-structures (grammar) from the asserting itself, one tries to delimit the latter according to its particular performance. Asserting has the peculiarity of at first analyzing a pregiven object, of delimiting in the analysis and therein of determining the whole.

One calls this determining that analyzes and delimits: thinking. Logic is the science of the fundamental structures of thinking. Logic as science has, like every science, sprung from philosophy, but it is in this just portrayed form itself philosophy no more. Logic quickly becomes, the more it develops, a mere learnable school subject. In it, general formulas and rules of thinking are treated. It is, therefore, appointed as *preparatory school* for all thinking, also in the individual sciences. Already with the collection of Aristotle's writings, the foundational writings (logic) were named οργανον, that is, fundamental tool for all thinking and knowing.

This logic that has been thus developed and grounded by Aristotle has maintained itself essentially unaltered in its main elements and character in a two-thousand year history up to the present day. What has been altered in the course of the history is the kind of leading-back-again of logic into philosophy, in each case according to the predominant kind and significance of the philosophical question. Furthermore, the manner of explanation of the rules of logic has changed. With regard to the leading-back-again, logic experiences essential rearrangements in the course of this history through Leibniz, Kant, Hegel, and recently in the so-called mathematical logic, which, however, never are such as to undermine the proper fundamental structure.

"That logic has taken this secure path already from the oldest times can be gathered from the fact that since *Aristotle* it has not been allowed to take a step backwards, if, to be sure, one does not want to credit it with improvement for doing away with a few dispensable subtleties or [a] clearer determination of what is presented, which, however, belong more to the elegance than to the certainty of the science. What is further remarkable about it is that it also has not been able to take any step forward and hence by all appearances seems to be self-contained and complete" (Kant, *Kritik der reinen Vernunft*, Preface to the 2nd edition, viii).

§ 3. The three common standpoints of the judgment about meaning, usefulness, and value of logic

We now ask: What can the occupation with this logic mean to us and [how can it] be even useful to us? What about the value of logic? The opinions about this are divided.

Some say: Through the knowledge of the logical fundamental structures, of the concepts and rules of thought, our thinking becomes conscious of its own process; the conscious process, however, offers the guarantee of a higher certainty and a greater acuteness. Every rule of the thought technique creates advantages and superiority.

The others say: The mere becoming familiar with prescriptions and rules does not yet give the guarantee of the right application on the right occasion. Far more fruitful is the practical exercise of the thought process. This can only be attained in the immediate execution in the individual sciences. We learn the thinking of physicists the best in the laboratory, juridical thinking the best in court trials, medical thinking at the sickbed. Who, moreover, does not bring along the ability to think to a certain degree will not attain it through the study of logic either, particularly because logic itself places especially high demands on thinking.

The third say: Let the study of logic be superfluous or even an obstacle, in any case, it is itself a legitimate task to reflect on the fundamental laws of thinking and thereby to experience what in a long history of the human spirit has been discerned about it. After all, "there must be more than meets the eye," if Kant, Hegel and others have incessantly troubled themselves over logic.

§ 4. The necessary task of a shaking up of logic

Whose position will we join? Well, no one's. We want to shake up logic as such from its outset, from its ground, to awaken and to make graspable an original task under this heading—not out of any whim or in order to bring something new, but because we *must*; and we must out of a necessity, which perhaps one or another among you will experience in the course of this semester. As long as we only quarrel over whether the hitherto existing logic may or may not be superfluous, we move, while we affirm it in this or that way, on the same level with it.

Admittedly, it thus appears that the adversaries of logic stand in certain superiority and go with us. But this is a delusion. By rejecting logic as an empty rule canon, nothing is accomplished. By getting out of the way of things of the mind, they are not yet overcome; they return with increased power and without our willing it. All of those who believe to be free in this regard move in the accustomed thought ways and thought procedures of this two thousand year old past.

So comes about the comical and already almost ridiculous spectacle that precisely the many mediocre people, who today take and formerly [have taken] the field against rationalism and intellectualism, blindly get stuck in it and founder in it.

Intellectualism is not overcome with mere grumbling, but through the hardness and severity of a completely new and secured thinking. It does not come overnight and [does] not [come] upon request. It does not come as long as [the] rule and might of the traditional logic are not broken from the ground up. That requires a battle in which our spiritual and historical destiny is decided, a battle for which we today do not even have the weapons and in which we today do not even know the adversary yet, so that we run the danger of inadvertently making common cause with the adversary, instead of attacking him. We must know that our spiritual history is bound 2,000 years back. This history is in its shaping power today still present, even if most have no inkling about it.

We retain for this battle the simple traditional word "logic." May the word be a reminder to us that our historical *Dasein*, and with this all confrontation, is sustained by the logic of the Greeks. May this name "logic" be a mandate for us to question in a more original and more encompassing manner after what intruded upon the Greeks through logic as the shaping power, as greatness of their historical *Dasein*, and what then assumed as western logic the rule over the spirit.

Only a long and painful detachment brings us into the open and prepares [us] to create the new form of discourse. We renounce every semblance of cheap superiority, which sees in logic only annoying formulas. We learn to take seriously the power of a thinking since long and its creative overcoming, without which a transformation of our *Dasein* will be baseless.

Of this willing, we understand that a remodeling of the sciences, if it is after all still possible, can only be accomplished thus: from a turning around of the attitude of knowing before all science. This turning around is only created through a long and unswerving execution of a revolution-izing questioning, a questioning that places us in the final decision.

The human being is dominated in similar ways by the powers of wisdom and error, being and semblance, and it is important not to play off one power against another, for precisely out of the disunion of both the human being receives his determination.

Logic is, therefore, for us, not a drill for a better or worse method of thought, but the questioning pacing off abysses of being, not the dried up collection of eternal laws of thought, but the place of the worthiness of question of the human being, his greatness. Logic is then, however, all the more no undisciplined idle talk about *Weltanschauung*, but sober-ing work that is bound in the genuine impulse and in essential need.

Recapitulation

We have begun by demonstrating to ourselves the traditional structure of logic. For logic, the proposition, the λόγος, the designating talk, is the fundamental phenomenon. Around it unfolds the system of that which presents itself as the later logic. In this connection, I have named four respects according to which, taken schematically, the fundamental structure develops.

1. Analysis into concepts, words, word meanings;
2. Assembly of the fundamental elements of the proposition and, fur-ther, of the proposition with another proposition in the connection of a syllogism;
3. Regulation for each of these structures (concept, proposition, judg-ment, syllogism) in the sense
   - of the principle of identity,
   - of the principle of non-contradiction,
   - of the principle of reason, in the positing of the connection of statements overall;
4. Formal consideration. It means that from the start one's eyes were fixed on these structures (concept, and so on) by disregarding the respective material content (the matter). One calls such a considera-tion, which in general disregards the matter, a formal consideration.

Thus arise rules for every possible thinking about every possible object in general. This structure that has developed academically in connection with philosophy, soon served as its support, soon again was absorbed into the central questions of philosophy and of knowledge in general. Logic, as it has been more or less boringly lectured to us in the schools and universities for a century, is subject to different value judgments.

1. Some say it is a formal schooling of thought.
2. The others regard it as completely useless, for thinking is to be learned only through concrete experience.
3. Again others say: The question of the practical use is not appropriate for logic. Logic has in itself as its own area of knowledge its own truth.

We do not express views on these questions because we do not expressly occupy ourselves with this logic. We stand rather before the fundamental task of shaking up this logic from top to bottom, not arbitrarily or out of obstinacy, with the intention of now erecting another logic. We stand before the shaking up of logic, which we do not undertake [in] 1934 perhaps with the purpose of an arbitrary "*Gleichschaltung*," but which we have been working on for ten years and which is grounded on a transformation of our *Dasein* itself, a transformation, which means the innermost necessity of our proper historical task. We are working on a shaking up, which we cannot will in the sense of a planning, but only out of the necessity of our fate.

The old title "logic" will be adhered to by us. For, our task does not release us from that which is given by the tradition. The title shall rather express for us that we bind ourselves to the creative confrontation with the tradition out of the awakening of original forces.

According to the general, already elucidated understanding, logic is the science of the formal fundamental structures and rules of thinking. We want to remind ourselves anew of this delimitation of the essence of logic and to question what really is put forward here.

First Part

The Question Concerning the Essence of Language as Fundamental and Guiding Question of All Logic

Logic is the science of λόγος, of talk, strictly taken, of language. If the thinking according to its fundamental structures and rules is logic, [if it] is investigated as a knowing about talking, then therein lies unspoken that thinking is in a certain sense a talking, a speaking. Now, to be sure, this conception from Greek philosophy was certainly at that time not substantiated further—and it is not up to today. Rather, the reversed conception is being advocated, that speaking represents only a form of expression and communication for thinking.

The question is not decided; it shall remain as question for us.

We can, however, say in general, without going into a particular definition of logic: Logic has to do in some sense with the λόγος as language. If thinking were a kind of language, then we could exaggeratedly say logic is a knowing about language. To be sure, this conception sounds at first strange. Whether it can be substantiated can only be decided in such a manner that we see how it stands in general with the relation of thinking and speaking. We cannot avoid the question concerning language and concerning the essence of language. The question concerning the essence of language is the fundamental question and the guiding question of all logic; one may, with this, delimit the concepts as one wants.

If we thus determine logic in advance in a stipulation, we take, as it were, the question concerning the essence of language as directive and guiding principle for the question concerning logic.

§ 5. Objections against the procedure of taking the question concerning
the essence of language as directive and guiding principle for the
question concerning logic

a) Language as object of the philosophy of language
The question concerning the essence of language is commonly the task
of philosophy of language; consequently, according to this stance, the
philosophy of language would be the vestibule of logic. By affirming
that the philosophy of language treats language as a theme of logic, we
have already inadvertently evaded that which we have posed to ourselves as task. Admittedly, we said, [the] task is the question concerning
the essence of language. If we, however, assert that this task is [the]
object of philosophy of language, then we have already suspended the
questioning—insofar as a particular proposition about the essence of
language has been already stipulated through this statement: namely,
that language may be something for the philosophy of language. We
have, with this, already entered into a definitive conception of language.

That is to say, philosophy of language can only be thought, if it is
distinguished from philosophy of religion, philosophy of history, political philosophy, philosophy of law, philosophy of art, and so on. These
entire philosophies are thereby at the same time coordinated with one
another within the whole, as one realm next to the other realm, as discipline within a comprehensive concept of philosophy from which the
character of this discipline is predetermined.

If we, therefore, assign language to a philosophy of language, then
we are immediately already seized by a certain determinate conception.
The questioning concerning language is fundamentally already thwart-
ed. For, perhaps it is a prejudice that language too is next to art, religion, the State, history, and so on, another area that one can investigate
in a special discipline.

We could reply: That is an empty dispute. Nevertheless, as matters stand, language is to be distinguished in a purely factual manner
from those areas (religion, nature, art, history, and so on) and thereby can itself be addressed as a special area. Perhaps it is such a special structure. Yet, if we remain true to our task, then that means that
we ask first whether language represents a special area or whether it
is something else, of which we up to today still have no concept.
Perhaps it is the other way around: That philosophy originates only

out of a sufficient understanding of language. We may not, therefore, force language and the questioning concerning it into the framework of a philosophy of language.

b) Narrowing of logic through language

Now, one could ask: Is it at all worthwhile that, with a view to a logic, we occupy ourselves at length with the essence of language? Surely, we are venturing into a certain area of knowledge, be it of philology or of general linguistics! Linguistics is a science, which is not the business of physicians, historians, and so on (physicians, only insofar as in a small corner, speech *disorders* are spoken of)—whereas logic is capable of being of interest to any scientific and any thinking human being. We thus come into the danger of intolerably narrowing the area so that it loses its general interest and only serves philology for a useful secondary consideration.

Such deliberations are natural and within certain limits also legitimate, as long as we remain accustomed to seeing the world in the partitioning of areas of science through the spectacles of faculties. However, this kind of seeing is in the right only under the presupposition that in general the whole of beings can be made accessible originally by way of the sciences.

This conception is an error. In philosophy, if anywhere, this error must be avoided. Philosophy searches for a knowing that, at the same time, is before all science and goes beyond all science; it searches for a knowing that is not necessarily bound to the sciences.

If we assess the question concerning the essence of language, whether from the field of vision of the lawyer as superfluous, or from that of the natural scientist as erroneous, or from that of the physician as unimportant, or from that of the philologist as deceitful, then we judge language and its essence, without having posed the question concerning it. However, in general, we call such a behavior, [such] a condemnation without previous careful questioning, recklessness, but here [we call it] a ridiculous arrogance of limited intellect that wants to be superior.

c) The secondary ranking of language: Language as means

However, even if we have the will to get free from this philistine judgment of things—something strange nevertheless remains in facing the question concerning the essence of language, in facing a question that evidently does not hold us in the center, but only leads to the edge and the surface. For language is, after all, obviously only a way for communication, a way for intercourse, an instrument of exchange, an instrument of representation; it is always only means for something else, always only that which is belated, that which is of secondary rank, hull and shell of things, but not their essence itself. This is what it looks like.

However, who would wish to contest that it is not so? Yet, we also hesitate to affirm that with this the essence of language is exhausted or even only met.

d) The grasping of language—preformed through logic

However, we want, to be sure, to inquire about the essence of language, that is, not commit ourselves to any explanation. Then, however, it is first requisite that language become accessible to us, be pregiven, as it were—in order to be able, then, to ask it what it may be. Where is language most palpable to us? A language is most securely put down in a dictionary and unfolded in grammar. The word forms of the dictionary stem, according to their definition, from grammar. Grammar creates the difference between word and statement, noun, verb, predicate, adjective, declarative statement, conditional statement, consecutive clause, and so on.

But now, this whole arrangement of language that is familiar to us has sprung from the fundamental determinations of logic; it has originated in the orientation to a specific language (the Greek language), in a specific kind of thinking, as it first prevailed in the Greek *Dasein*.

Thus, we stand before the facts that now logic, for which we first wanted to create the vestibule by making language a topic, itself is the site of origin of language. Our questioning concerning the essence of language with a view to logic becomes a helpless undertaking. We turn in a circle insofar as every access to language is already determined by logic.

If we take together all that has been said so far, it becomes clear that this questioning concerning the essence of language, though it looks clear-cut, immediately entangles itself in the greatest difficulties:

1. Language is shoved aside into a particular area of objects.
2. Language is shoved aside into a realm that does not appear to be as comprehensive as the formal thinking of logic.

3. Language is secondary insofar as it is only means of expression.
4. The grasping of language is preformed for us through the predominant logic.

§ 6. The two manners of questioning. The character of the question of the essence as fore-question and the three respects of the question of the essence

If we think that through, we slowly become puzzled over our task of asking about the essence of language. We must try to escape this danger of premature commitment. We must keep ourselves open for the essence of language. In other words: questioning and questioning is not the same. Questioning is not a rattling on, some kind of announcement of created thoughts, nor unsteady staggering in doubts, but proper and genuine questioning has its own discipline [*Disziplin, d.h. Zucht*]. Genuine, that is, essential questioning is sustained by that dark bidding, from which a questioning arises, over which the individual who poses the question for the first time has no control; for that, the individual becomes only the passage for the history of a *Volk* guided by that radiating restlessness, which in order to be truly endured demands severity of bearing and genuine disposition. For the philistine in the field of knowing, the hard will of the questioning is uncomfortable. For the middle class of the spirit, every long and the longest worthiness of question immediately becomes decay and thereby suspicious. That is completely in order and also can never be changed.

It does not follow from this that the philistine alone is the standard for what is genuine, [for] what is essential and what [is] not essential. The true questioning requires the calling and the formation and the long education and practice. For that reason, the most beautiful talking about the questioning remains useless as well. The questioning is practiced only in a questioning manner in a long endurance of essential questions.

We now take up again our question concerning the essence of language and remind ourselves that the change of logic into the general task of the question concerning the essence of language thrusts us into a medley of things worthy of question. It is now important to withdraw ourselves from these constantly intrusive prejudices about the essence of language, even if this gives the impression of running away from the veiled essence of language and setting out into a retreat. To be sure, a peculiar retrogression is necessary above all —a retrogression, which each, who takes a run before leaping far, runs back. For, there is no gradual and steady crossing from the unessential into the essential. Each one must leap for himself; nobody can be relieved from it, not even through the ever so genuine and indispensable community. Each must himself venture the leap, if he wants to be a member of a community.

We shall and want to make this questioning effective and thus must procure in outline sufficient clarity regarding the motivating force of such a questioning and of its character so that we will be able to achieve jointly this striding of the questioning.

Every question of the essence has the character of a fore-question, and this can be characterized in three respects:

1. Every question of the essence is a fore-question [*Vorfrage*] in the sense that it is an advancing [*Vorgehen*] in the manner of an attack that creates an alley, paves a way, in general first of all unlocks a realm whose borders, direction, and dimension remain for long in the dark. For our topic that means: Whither do we ask, if we inquire about language? What about language? What kind of being [*Art zu sein*] does a language have? Is language actually put down in the dictionary? Or elsewhere? Is there in general something like language in general? Or is always one's own language, the historical language, essential? If yes: why and in how far?

2. Every question of the essence is a fore-question in the sense that it not only leaps forward [*vorspringt*] into the whole of the essence, but in a questioning manner draws out by questioning, moves out distinctive traits of this essence. For language that means: What belongs to a language? What makes it inwardly possible? What is the ground of the possibility? Where does this ground [*Grund*] become an abyss [*Abgrund*]?

3. Every question of the essence is a fore-question in the sense that it not only thrusts toward the front [*vorne*], but [also] at the same time precedes [*vorhergeht*] every individual and separate questioning in the respective realm. In each philosophy and linguistics, in each field of discourse, in each bearing of the human being lies unpronounced already a distinctive answer to the question concerning the essence of language.

The fore-question has consequently a threefold sense:
1. It questions ahead [*nach vorne*].
2. It questions forth [*hervor*] the fundamental structure.
3. It precedes [*geht vorher*].

The fore-question, as distinguished from that which we commonly call question, is fundamentally never settled. If the question of the essence ever counts as settled, then the decline and the boundless misinterpretation have already begun. Philosophizing is nothing other than constant being underway in this fore-field of the fore-questioning.

Recapitulation

We carry through our task under the traditional title "logic" and [we] want to indicate with this that this task is no arbitrary renewal, but, though in itself new, is nevertheless only the execution of necessities, which lie in the unfolding of the western spirit.

It is necessary to make clear what lies in the fact that the discipline *logic*, which counts as science of *thinking*, actually grasps thinking as λóγος. Thinking understood in the sense of *talking*—this remarkableness is for us decisive. Thinking is here conceived in the sense of talking and speaking. Though that was the fact, it has today dwindled down to the last remnants.

We hold tight to the old fact in the sense that we determine logic as *question* concerning the essence of λóγος, of language in the widest sense. From this, it follows for the usual interpretation that the treatment of the topic, so to speak, is shifted to a philosophy of language. With this, however, a double fore-decision has been reached:

1. A special area is enclosed in itself, as opposed to the areas State, religion, art, and so on.
2. The area and its kind of method are assigned to a philosophy, to a system, that is somehow predetermined.

On account of this handicap, we cannot, if we, as actual questioners, want to question, if we want to leave open the question concerning the essence of language, from the start tolerate the philosophy of language and the formulation of linguistic-philosophical questions.

A further deliberation lay there in that with this formulation of the question concerning language we narrow logic (as opposed to thinking).—However, the questioning concerning language means a narrowing of logic, only if one regards language from the point of view of a special science (Faculty), if one believes that the worth and unworthiness of a thing, of a state of affairs, can be decided from a science. That is a mistake! Philosophy is something other than science.

Finally, we must also consider that language, even if one wanted to place it according to the breadth of its domain on a par with thinking, still remains something of a secondary rank: a means of expression, only hull and shell.

Finally, the moment we attempt to ask about language, following the way of natural science, we run against the dictionary and grammar—in order, then, to ascertain that all of grammar derives itself from the Greek logic, which determines the fundamental concepts and rules of speaking and saying. We get in the strange position that we, on the one hand, free ourselves from logic only to arrive, on the other hand, again in the fetters of logic.

The questioning concerning the essence is not self-evident; it cannot be put in motion at will, for it has its very own character. Three directions are peculiar to it:

1. The question of the essence is a fore-question [*Vorfrage*] in the sense that it leads the way [*vorgeht*], forces its way, opens an area, within which what is asked about belongs.
2. The question of the essence is a fore-question in the sense that, in this fore-thrusting [*Vorstoßen*], it, at the same time, questions forth [*hervorfragt*] the first references from that which is inquired, the first features, the contour—and thereby illuminates what belongs, for example, to language, wherein the ground of its being subsists.
3. The question of the essence is fore-question insofar as it precedes [*vorausgeht*] all specific questioning. In any historical (or natural scientific) formulation of the question, a *fore-conception* of history, nature, and so on, lies unpronounced.

These fore-questions can never count as settled. The minute the question concerning the essence counts as settled, a door is opened to unessence. Philosophizing is nothing else than the constant being underway in the fore-field of the fore-questions.

If we thus attempt to question what philosophy may be, what language, what art may be, what *Volk* [may be], in that way, we thereby always touch at something great within the *Dasein* of the human being, at one such that surmounts and, at the same time, confuses the individual human being.

All that is great in the *Dasein* of the human being is, at the same time, also small, at the same time, diminished and, with that, ambiguous. The average everyday of the human being needs this diminution, the everyday needs this mediocrity; otherwise, the human being could not exist in this everyday. It is a misunderstanding to want to eliminate the mediocrity; it is necessary for the individual and for a *Volk*; it is also not dangerous, if one grasps it in its limits. It is only dangerous when the small is even further diminished by it, if one forgets to demand of oneself reverence and severity for the things. The great is retained only if the human being succeeds in magnifying the great, that is, in demanding severity of himself in the face of the great. This holds also for that which we now take into question, for language.

First Chapter

The Question Concerning the Essence of Language

We begin with the question of the essence, therefore, with the fore-questions. We ask: Whither does something like language belong? Is there such a thing like language anywhere?

§ 7. Language—preserved in the dictionary

We said in the previous lesson, language is captured and preserved in the dictionary. Indeed, a dictionary is something of language, namely, an enormous amount of individual pieces and shreds of language. We say *Wörterbuch* [dictionary], there are in it words [Trans.: or "terms": *Wörter*] and not words [*Worte*], nothing spoken. These words are now, however, not isolated at all, not in disorder, chaotically muddled; they are ordered in the sequence of the alphabet, compared to which the spoken word sequence is certainly something entirely different. This sum of words in the dictionary belongs in a certain sense to language.

If we now, however, concede that this sum of words belongs to the stock of language—how large is the scope? Are all words in the dictionary? Is it possible to confine language to a specific number of words? Or does language form ever new, and sheds, on other the hand, spoken words and words that then suddenly disappear? Which condition of language shall be actually grasped in a dictionary? Is not a dictionary like an ossuary at the cemetery, where bones and remnants of bones of different humans from long ago are neatly piled up so that precisely through this arrangement the whole destruction becomes manifest?

§ 8. Language as event in the dialogue

It is clear: We do not find language in the dictionary, even if the whole stock is registered there. Language is only there, where it is spoken, where it happens, that is, among human beings. We will here look around in order to experience where and how a language is as language.

So, the one speaks with the other; they enter into conversation. Forthwith, they part and speak no longer. Does language now cease to be? Or perhaps in the meantime, somewhere on another occasion, other human beings speak with one another? Language leaps over thus to a certain extent from one group to another, [it] is thus constantly in change. There will always be many who are not speaking when others are speaking. When and where now is this language? Perhaps only there, where all human beings of a language community speak at the same time? Is language here whole and actual? Or can a language never be actual in this sense, but always only fragmentarily, so that [it] does not happen at all that a language is?

Let us suppose that the case happens that all human beings of a language community speak this language at the same time. Would it be thereby guaranteed that now too the whole language is spoken, that the whole language comes up for discussion? Presumably, indeed, most certainly, much would thereby remain unspoken; language would be spoken only in special respects, for example, as colloquial language. As poetry, for example, language would remain entirely unrealized; it would thus again not be itself in its full being.

But, even assuming this: Language would be actually spoken according to all of its directions and possibilities, and were the thrust of an earthquake now immediately to take place so that the whole community was numbed mute by fear, would language then cease to be?

Is language only then, when it is spoken? Is it not, when one is silent? Or is a language not at all, but arises again and again at the moment of speaking? Then it would be constantly becoming and passing, [it] would have no being, but would be a becoming. It remains then, to be sure, to question whether this becoming is not precisely also a being. Assuming that we must address all that is not nothing, as what is or [as] being [als ein Seiendes oder Sein], then language also *is*, even if it itself constantly *becomes*.

Where, when and how is a language? We said of our own accord: first there, where it is spoken, first then, when it is spoken. We see now that this declaration is ambiguous to the highest degree, [it is], above all, worthy of question.

If we look around in the philosophy of language and there perhaps search for explanation in the individual systems, [of] how one thinks the being of a language, then we search in vain for the answer, for the question is not at all posed there. The neglect of this fore-question is why the speculation over language in the philosophy of language hovers around groundlessly and hacks around in the void; precisely this neglect leads to a series of familiar fictitious problems.

§ 9. Language—determined from the kind of being of the human
     being. The answer of metaphysics

Against our objection that the being of language is unquestioned and undetermined, an opposition arises. One replies, the kind of being of language is already secured. We have, after all, ourselves sufficiently secured where we search for the being of language. Language is a human activity. The kind of being of this activity will be determined from the kind of being of the human being, for the human being alone, as distinguished from stone, plant and animal, speaks. The being of the human being holds in itself the being of language.

And what is the human being? That one knows for a long time. The human being (says Greek philosophy) is ζῷον λόγον ἔχον. The Latin says: *Homo est animal rationale*, the human being is a living being, that is, a rational one.

The human being is, therefore, in this mode of being, firstly as living being, distinguished from all the inanimate (from mere matter), as something animate. He has, in some sense, the mode of being of life. However, he is, in distinction from something animate, distinguished within what is animate (plants, animal), namely as rational (λόγον ἔχον). The human being is that living being that has language at his disposal, that possesses language. This to us long since familiar, but faded determination of the essence of the human being was thus achieved with the Greeks with regard to language, with reference to the fact that language distinguishes the being of the human being.

But what now? We just said after all: the being of language, which is enigmatic and dark, shall be clarified from the being of the human being. Now we say conversely, the being of the human being is determined with reference to the being and essence of language. That is a very awkward situation; that is evidently a turning-oneself-in-a-circle.

And, if we now do not evade this circular movement and do not remove it with some paltry information, if we rather put this peculiar fact of the circle into effect, we come in time to a distinctive draft that arises around the circle. This circling gradually becomes a vortex. This vortex draws us slowly into an abyss, but only just then, when we do not evade from the start this moving in a circle. We can do that of course; nobody can hinder us. We still have the choice. We can dodge, entirely unhindered, the question of what the human being is, [we] can, at the same time, perhaps still guess with others, chatter with others about the essence of the human being, [we] can, at the same time, attend to our sciences and make sure that we are being heard and pass our exams, [we] can execute our duties and become a useful member of the community of the *Volk*.

In doing this, we can encounter the opinion that a questioning in which the human being looks behind itself is sick, that it is now rather the time to free oneself of reflection and to start acting. To be sure: Such questioning is an obstacle, it disturbs the sleep, and nothing is better than a healthy sleep. [Heavy stomping.] [Trans.: The previous brackets appear in the original text.] For what do we need to know and to question what the human being is? The human being is, anyway, entirely laden with knowledge. The human being is precisely he who knows. The human being is in the manner of knowing—and does not know what he himself is.

We can take that as a simple assessment and can go over to the everyday course of the day. We can, however, also sense from this assessment that the human being knows and does not know who he himself is; an uncanny judgment. An uncanniness that loses nothing by the fact that those who are the happy-go-lucky human beings have no inkling of it. We can let the question rest, but we can also ask the question: Both are in our power because it rests in our freedom. The decision passes one way or another, depending on whether we take seriously or not that which we are as human beings.

If we now ask the question concerning the essence of language, we are asking about the essence of the human being. We see already now more clearly that this question concerning the essence of language is in fact no question of philology and of philosophy of language, but a need of the human being, assuming that the human being takes the human being seriously.

By deciding for this question, we are not outside of the predicament of the formulation of the question, outside of the remarkable circle. Is there any way here to make headway in the discussion of this connection?

Perhaps we do not need at all to pose the question concerning language beforehand as a separate one, but can take together human being and language and ask about the human being as the speaking human being. This starting point hits after all in a certain way upon the proper facts of the being of the human being. We thus investigate, accordingly, what sort of a being is the human being.

Second Chapter

The Question Concerning the Essence of the Human Being

The question concerning the essence of language has unexpectedly broadened into the question: "What is the human being?" However, now begins the same difficulty that we have already encountered with the fore-question. Language, to be sure, is not now hanging in the air, but belongs to the being of the human being. Yet, where does the human being belong? Where does the human being stand in the whole of being?

Here also, we can again pause with this questioning and give the explanation that this question is already decided for eternity by the Old and New Testament. We must then, however, put this explanation into effect. If it wants to be taken seriously, we must state that this explanation is an explanation of faith, and with that and from now on, we must actually believe and not pretend surreptitiously, as if we were asking.

The essence of the human being can, however, also be and remain truly questionable, even if only *in such a manner* that we face, undecidedly and helplessly, different answers to the question concerning the essence of the human being—answers perhaps of the following kind: The human being is within the course of evolution the most highly developed mammal and primate and thus the outermost branch of earth history in the natural phylogenetic tree of life. This answer wants to step forward, even if it has perhaps already has become impossible as an answer by natural philosophy.

Or it is said: The human being is creative retrospective look of nature upon itself (Schelling); the human being is a beast of prey (Spengler); the human being is something that must be overcome

(Nietzsche); the human being is a sick animal, a wrong way, a blind alley, in which the stream of life has finally gone astray.

Therefore: what is the human being?

Recapitulation

We repeat the course of the preceding in order to win back the position and the direction. Logic remains that which deals with the λόγος for us as well. But, we do not persist blindly in the conception of the preceding western history of the spirit. Logic is not the mere combining of formulas and rules of thinking, but logic is for us a questioning. For that reason, we may not classify the concept and the essence of the λόγος from the start in a specific conception.

In general, λόγος must, first of all, be designated as talk, as speaking. Hence, we ask first of all concerning the essence of language, but not in a philosophy of language, which degrades language to a specific separate area. We do not take language as something of a secondary rank, perhaps as a means for communication. Nor is grammar the first and decisive way of grasping language. We ask about the essence of language. Logic is the question concerning the essence of language. Logic is never an antiquated and dried-up school subject. Rather, logic is for us the name for a task, the task, namely, of preparing the coming generation so that it will again become a knowing one, such a one that it is knowingly and wants to know and can be truly knowing.

For that end, science is not needed. That knowing lies before and, at the same time, beyond science. For that reason, the decision about science is not reached in science and its branches; it is decided in and with philosophy, with the question of whether or not we summon the power of an original knowing about the essence of things.

This preparation [*Vorbereitung*] of the readiness [*Bereitschaft*] of a genuine knowing serves the forthcoming logic. We ask about the essence of language. The question of the essence is, however, in itself always a fore-question that is a fore-question in a threefold sense:

1. That it questions ahead [*nach vorne*], unlocks a question realm,
2. That it questions forth [*hervorfragt*] the determination of the essence,
3. That it already always lies in front [*vor...liegt*] of the concrete questions and is co-determining.

We have begun to pose the question of the essence as fore-question: Whither belongs such a thing as language? We started out in this connection from the obvious. Language is put down in the dictionary and grammar. In the dictionary, we find a certain stock-taking of terms, yet only as a collection of mortal remains. Never do we grasp there the living language. The living language is a speaking.

Hence, the further question is: what is speaking? And which speaking constitutes the reality of language? Is language then real, if only this one or that one speaks, or is it real, when all members of a linguistic community speak at the same time? Does it cease to be, if one is silent?

To search for the reality of language in speaking is perhaps more promising than the search in the dictionary. Yet, the indication that language rests in the human being, does not satisfy, as long as we do not know *how* and *where* this speaking is. This speaking happens among human beings. It is a human activity. Language is a characteristic of the human being. If we pose the question in its entire dimension, we thus arrive at the question: What is the human being? The answer to this question was already given in antiquity: ἄνθρωπος ζῷον λόγον ἔχον. The human being is that living being that disposes over language.

We are thus in a strange situation. We find language first determined from the essence of human being—and then the essence of the human being again from language. We are here in the peculiar situation of circular movement. How shall we find the way out of the circle? Not at all! We shall not find the way out, but *remain* in the circle and set going this vortex movement.

It is the peculiarity of the thinking that philosophizes that it moves in a vortex, which leads into the abyss. Philosophy is always in a vortex. In science, on the other hand, the object is objectively present-at-hand; we always stand opposite it in a certain manner, but never arrive at a philosophical formulation of a question with this.

One thing is clear: We must couple the question "What is language?" with the question "What is the human being?" We tried to pose the question "What is the human being?" and, at the same time, we have seen that we can refer to different answers. The answer of the Old and New Testaments is, to be sure, only understood as answer in the sense of faith. We can, however, also let the essence of the human being be worthy of question. If we look back to the more recent history, we thus find the human being determined in biology, as the latest and outermost branch of the phylogenetic tree in the earth history, in romanticism, as creative retrospective look of nature upon itself, in Spengler, as a predatory animal, or in Nietzsche, as "that which must be overcome."

What is the human being? From where shall we take the answer? The question obviously does not let itself be answered without further ado through discussion of an empty concept of the human being. For, even such a concept is always drawn from a specific experience of the human being. We must, therefore, look around in the different forms of life, races, cultures, *Weltanschauungen*, and eras. If we do that, do we then know what the human being is? We can, if need be, arrange together varieties of humanity, arrange a kind of herbarium. We can then see that this and that human being belongs under this or that type. However, the question of what now is the human being is not answered with this. We say, to be sure, only what kind of human being is precisely this human being. That is no answer to the question concerning the essence of the human being.

§ 10. The right launching of the fore-question.
      What- and who-question

I have already mentioned that the question of the essence has the character of a fore-question. That means that with the question of the essence it is not indifferent as to how and in which direction the question is launched; it is not indifferent whether the direction is kept to, whether we from the start adequately meet [*treffen*] at the first attempt or whether the question remains underdetermined in the formulation of a question. The fore-question must satisfy all three conditions, it must genuinely launch and sufficiently determine in order to remain question-strong for the additional questions and not become overpowered by a haphazard answer.

How are we in our case, however, to get in the situation of asking this question wrongly? But, of course, we are asking unprejudiced: "What is the human being?" However, even with this question we have already asked wrongly—that is, insofar as we are asking: "*What* is the human being?" With this, we designate the human being in advance as an object, a thing, as something we encounter, encounter and come upon as present-at-hand, organize according to kind and species, and display according to the order. Yet, how else are we to take the questioning fore-view of the human being as long as we are asking for his essence? The essence of a matter surely does mean that *what* something is. Surely, every being has an essence!

Yet, not every essence lets itself be determined as *what-being*, namely, not in those cases when already the question concerning the *what* constantly shoves us aside in its course of question, instead of bringing us nearer to the beings concerned—and with this turns our questioning into a passing-by-questioning.

We must decide whether we are moving in such a passing-by-questioning, if we ask: "What is the human being?" Is there not still another form of questioning? Certainly! Instead of asking, *"What* is the human being?" we can ask, *"How* is the human being?" That can mean, how is he constituted? Which is his manner of being?

Now, it is easy to see that the question "How is the human being?" always traces itself back to the question, "What is the human being?" *How* such a thing like a mountain, a number, and so on is, determines itself from that *what* the respective being is. The How-question does not release us from the what.

There remains no other possibility of posing the question of the essence concerning the human being, as long as we do not realize in how far this question is a wrong question in relation to the human being. Every question, and the question of the essence in a particular sense, arises in the face of what appears strange to us. The strangeness, however, is not removed through the questioning. We let that which is strange come over us in the questioning, but not to come over us so that we are swallowed up in it. We face up to the strange.

If we now encounter in our realm something like a human being as something strange, *how* do we ask toward him? We ask not indeterminately *what*, but *who* he is. We inquire about and experience the human being, not in the realm of the *Thus* or *What*, but in the realm of *such* and *such* [*des* Der *und* Der, *der* Die *und* Die], of the *We*.

The question of the essence is a fore-question. The genuine and fitting fore-questioning is not the *What*-question, but the *Who*-question. We do not ask," *What* is the human being?", but *"Who* is the human being?" This seems to be a mere matter of words, and, yet, with this formulation of the question, a definite course is already given to the answer.

In the pursuit of the course of this question, the essence of the human being must now light up to us, as it were, at the first glimmer. The queried one responds to the question "I" or, if there are several, "we." Or one answers with a proper name. The fore-question thus always is, "Who are you?"—"Who are [plural] you?"—"Who are we?"

§11. The human being as a self

The We, the [plural] You, the You, the I are what is asked about. Human beings are thus pregiven to us at the launching as We and [plural] You and I and You. To the question of how the We and [plural] You and I and You are to be determined, we could respond, they are, as distinguished from plants, animals, stones, and so on, *persons* and associations of persons. However, what shall we understand by the title "person"? Apart from the fact that I and You, [plural] You and We are not unambiguous and at once clear in their origin, we must ascertain that with this answer we have already deviated from the course of the question into the *What*-question, for we tried to determine *what* is the You and I and [plural] You and We. We must, however, hold the course of the *Who*-question and try to ask, who comes to meet us out of this course of the question.

Who are you? Who are you yourself? Who am I myself? Who are we ourselves? The Who-question aims toward the realm of such being, which is at any given time respectively a self. We can now grasp the answer to the fore-question thus: The human being is a *self.*

If only we now knew what a self is. Here, we entirely lack the concept. To be sure, we surmise, in a completely unclear manner, a certain sense. We understand what *We ourselves, You yourself, I myself* mean. However, the determination of the essence always demands the concept. In this way, the answer binds that which is strange only temporarily. The strange, therefore, has not waned away completely; on the contrary.

That which is strange does not lie in the fact that we have no definition of the self, but that we in our questioning have already gone astray twice from the course. We kept to the course, insofar as we asked no more "what," but "who." The answer, "he himself," is correct, insofar as we assert what has resulted for us in the course of the question. It is nevertheless *untrue*, for it veils from us what properly lies included in it. In science in general, we know how to say much that is *correct*, but very little that is *true*. Science moves mostly within the circumference of what is correct and not of what is true.

In how far, however, is the answer that is correct in itself, "The human being is a self," nevertheless untrue. Because we do not *keep up* the question, we do not answer out of the course that the question points out. "Who is the human being?"—A self. "Who is a self?"— We! "Who are we, therefore, who are we, we, the questioners?"

The fore-question is based on the human being as a self. The answer refers to the questioner, *to his self. We ourselves* are the inquired. If the questioner asks, who the human being is as a self, he himself becomes the queried one. Therefore, the question reads, not "What is the human being?" and not "Who is the human being?", but "Who are we ourselves?"

This cuts off once and for all that we ask about types, eras, cultures. We ask concerning what is asked about in the question. Only then do we first take the correct answer as true answer, if we do not forget the question included in this answer, if we do not misunderstand the answer as *what*-determination, as property, but as instruction to the self, namely, to ourselves.

Who are we ourselves? That slowly becomes distinct, if we step-by-step and rigorously ask the question concerning the essence of the human being completely. The peculiar difficulty results from this. No wonder that the question concerning the human being has developed so little hitherto *as question*, no wonder that the answers are so confused, haphazard, and aimless. For, one labyrinth after another lurks on the way. It is not only the case that we forget at once the truth of the answer in the correctness of the answer—we misunderstand time and again the true inner order and sequence of the question.

It seems as if the question "What is a self?" were correct. We already see, however, in the question form "What is...?" that we already question-away again from the course. Admittedly, we shall see that the question "What is the self?" is correct at a certain position of the course of the question, but only at a certain position—and only then, if we have sufficiently developed the course of the question.

Nevertheless, we can now at first make do without the *concept* of the self. We have supplied the proof for this. That is to say, we have understood the question, insofar as it concerns us. We have a fore-understanding of the word and its meaning, though a *non-conceptual* one; we cannot define it at the first go. Insofar as we head for the concept, we name the fore-understanding a *fore-conceptual* one. The answer "The human being is a self" unveils itself to us as [a] question that takes course toward *ourselves*.

We remain exposed for the whole passage of the question "Who are we?", and the more truly we ask through it, the more obstinately will each further-question return to ourselves. That is why we do not advance further with this, but encircle ourselves ever nearer and more sharply.

a) The I—determined through the self, not conversely

The questioners, who ask this question, are now placed in the question, they become worthy of question. We ask: "Who are we ourselves?" Each one of us is he himself, and as such he is an I-Myself, and thus is shown that we ourselves, as the composition, as it were, as the multitude of many I-Myself, as the multitude of separate Is, have thereby led the self back to the I. Each one of us is a self, because he is an I. The essence of the self is grounded in the essence of the I, self-hood in the I-ness.

This I, ego, one grasps, since Descartes, as subject and subjectivity, as subject that stands opposite the object and objectivity. This I is res cogitans. With Kant, the I is *consciousness* of something or of itself, in a wider sense, *reason*, a determination that was grasped in the further development as spirit.

Along such a way, we have again reached the initial determination: to the rendition of the I as subject, as consciousness, reason, spirit. That is not only here in the lecture a formal conceptual development, but it has been the course of the development of the self-understanding of the human being of modernity.

With this consideration, we have now strayed anew from our question, namely, immediately at the beginning of the new approach. We said: each one of us is he himself and as such an I-Myself. This proposition is not only untrue, but this time the proposition is even incorrect, insofar as the self is led back to the I-Myself and thus to the I.

Certainly, each one of us is an I-Myself; he is, however, precisely also formally a You-Yourself, not only in the other You who addresses him, but also by addressing himself (for example, "You have done that wrongly" [said to oneself] [Trans.: The brackets appear in the original text.]). Each I is for this reason not only a You-Yourself, in which an I-Myself speaks, but also a We-Ourselves and You-Yourselves.

The self is no distinguishing determination of the I. This is the fundamental error of modern thinking. The self is not determined from the I, but the self-character belongs just as well to the You, to the We, and to the [plural] You. The self is enigmatic in a new manner. The self-character does not belong separately to the You, to the I, to the We, but to all that in [a] similar original manner. It will have to be asked whether and in how far we may be able to push forward into the essence of the self and, with this, into the essence of the human being with this launching.

Recapitulation

The guiding question of logic, as we want to understand it, reads: "What is language?" This question has led us back to the question, "What is the human being?" This question has the character of the fore-question. The launching of the question must be directed so that which is asked about is struck in advance. We saw that the question "What is the human being?" misses the course of the question. The question concerning the human being must transform itself from the What-question into the Who-question. For the What-question conceives the human being as a present-at-hand thing.

"Who is the human being?"—in this kind of asking, the human being is met at first insofar as we perhaps call out with the "Who" to a stranger who is coming up to us. We are now no longer in the danger of underdetermining this "Who" in the further continuation.

The question "Who is the human being?" leads us to the next answer. If we ask a certain human being "Who are you?" we thus receive as answer "I." And if we ask several, we thus receive as answer "we." Or we receive a proper name as answer. We grasp this I, You, We, [plural] You as person and association of persons. This answer is, however, already again a mistake, insofar as we do not determine what is asked about from itself, but on the ground of a certain respect as living being and as rational. If we unambiguously head straight for that which is asked about, then we ask: "Who are you yourself?"—"Who is he himself?"—"Who am I myself?" Those who are asked about are, therefore, in each case a *self*.

It has to be asked further: "What is a self?" With this, however, we stand already again outside of the course of the question. We must again conceive *the human being* as a self. Hence, the question reads: "Who is he himself—the questioner?"—"Who are we ourselves—the questioners?"

The question of the essence concerning the human being has in a peculiar manner placed in the question the one who questions with the one who is questioned. The questioner is here always also affected by the question. With this, it must be connected that we run the danger of slipping off the course of question, not only in the beginning, but again and again; we run the danger of falling back into the What-question, but in doing so also attempting a determination of the essence, which is carried out within the horizon of the what-concept.

For this reason, it is required to hold to the course of the question toward the *self* and the *Who*. That seems to be easy, since we ourselves seem, after all, to be those closest to ourselves. Who are we ourselves? Each one of us is an I-Myself, the many I together are a We. The self leads itself back to the I.

Thereby, we arrive at the determination of the I as foundation, which played its role in modern philosophy. This orientation of the questioning toward the human being as the I was possible because one missed, respectively, did not know, the question concerning the essence of the self. To be sure, each one of us is an I-Myself, but also just as well a You-, a We-, a [plural] You-yourself. The character of selfhood is no distinguishing determination of the I, but the human being as himself is above all I and You and We and [plural] You and equally original.

It must be emphasized: The human being is not a self because he is an I, but the converse: He can only be an I because he is in essence a self. The He-Himself is neither limited to the I, nor reducible to the I. Hence, from the rightly understood self, no way leads to the I as essential ground; otherwise, the self would remain in the I-likeness and in representation.

b) The [plural] You and We—determined through the self,
   not through the mere plurality

The fact that the human being is he himself entails a manifold belongingness of the human beings among one another and with one another
as You and I. Here too, we have no subsequent crowd of several, many,
individualized Is, just as little as the [plural] You is a crowd, a mass of
our You. We cannot even add ourselves up as isolated I to a sum total,
to a We. If I say "I and I and I," I do not get away from the I, I only
always repeat myself. We can only say "I and you and you." But even
that is after all never a mere count. I say, for example "I and you and
you." That can mean: I as belonging to [plural] you. In this sense then, I
say better "you and you and I." (However, I can certainly also say "I
and you and you.")

But even if I *say* "you and you and I," there still *is* a We: We, who
stand under a certain mandate, who find ourselves in a special situation.
If I say "I and you and you," then that means that the I is placed opposite the [plural] You: a relationship of standing-opposite, for example,
for lecturer and audience, better: a relationship of leading-the-way and,
spoken here from the point of the students, of sitting opposite, of going
along or perhaps also not going along. In this reciprocal relationship of
the I and [plural] You, there lies a peculiar relationship of reference.

Nor is this [plural] You, in return, the sum total of individual Yous.
It is not the number of many You that amounts to the [plural] You, such
as one and one and one and one amount to four. It is rather conversely:
The belongingness to the lecture is that which is essential; it is grounded in the listening-together, in the inclusiveness of the individuals in
the audience. This [plural] You of the listener is divided in the [plural]
You, which as such, from such relationship, are addressed.

However, supposing now there is only a single listener, then there
is, of course, only one You; and if a second listener is added, then the
You has turned into a [plural] You based on the number, from the two!
That is correct and is nevertheless untrue. I will not say as teacher
"you" and "[plural] you," but "you" and "[deferential] you there." The
You and the [deferential] you there do *not* yield the [plural] You. In the
[plural] You lies the You of the audience. This comes about when the
second one listens too and not only audits. If that does not happen, then
the [plural] You of the audience remains limited to one You.

The audience determines itself not owing to the fact that one or ten or three hundred are there. All of these determine themselves as listener first owing to the fact that they listen too, belong to the audience. Only in it [the audience] is there a numerical more opposite the You.— However, is not "[plural] You" still a plural in opposition to a singular? This number-like, numerical plus is in a certain sense a necessary, but no sufficient, condition for the change from the You to the [plural] You. This "plus one" does not constitute the essence of the change.

However, even this concession of the meaning of the numerical for the distinction of You from [plural] You is not necessary and does not concern the state of affairs. The living language in an organized and historically rooted community, perhaps on the farmstead, creates the true references. A young farmer on the stead will not say: "Grandfather, you look tired," but "[deferential] You look tired." The grandfather is only a single one, but a unique one, who needs no second one in order to be addressed with "[plural] You." It would be completely erroneous to believe the "[plural] You" were to express a less intimate and close relationship opposite the "you." That would be a misunderstanding. The nearness of human beings to one another does not coincide with the degree of intimacy. Conversely, we can say: "[plural] You, my fellow Germans," and the "[plural] You" transforms itself immediately into a: "You, my *Volk*." It has a peculiar relationship with the change of the singular into the plural.

The [plural] You is thus not originally determined through the number, but through the respective character of the self that is here addressed. Assuming that I use the [plural] You in the sense of addressing a plurality of human beings, then those addressed are reduced with this to mere numbers. This reduction in this [plural] You takes those addressed not as they themselves, but as a crowd of arbitrary conceived ones. Yet, even if I say "[plural] you" to a crowd in this degrading manner, then the [plural] You remains still related to and grounded in the self. Even the human crowd, which, for example, congregates at a car accident, is never a mere sum of present-at-hand human beings. Even the dull and steaming mass [of people] remains in its manner still a self.

On the other hand, the [plural] You of a genuine audience can deteriorate into a specific amount of denumerable booklets, perhaps at the treasurer's office of the university. To be sure, also those who are represented by the booklets are still addressed by the civil servants as "[plural] you," but as specific numbers in the rubric of the professor's lecture.

That may suffice for a first explanation of the statement: The We is just as little a sum of I as the [plural] You is a sum of you. If many I are together and each I says by himself "I, I," then out of the plurality precisely the opposite of the We originates, in any case from the proper We. However, even this shattered We is no mere sum, but a definitive manner of the We-ourselves.

We infer positively from this that in the [plural] You and We what is decisive is not the number-like, but the self-character. The character of the self is peculiar neither to the I nor to the You, neither to the We nor to the [plural] You in a predominant sense. The character of the self lies in a certain way *beyond* and *before* all I, You, We, [plural] You. In which way, that remains the question.

c) Is the self the species of the I, You, We, [plural] You?

One is now inclined to say that the character of selfhood befits the I-Myself as such, the You-Yourself as such, the We-Ourselves as such. With that, the self is that which is common to all of that which is named. We want to elucidate this relationship of the self to the I, You, We, [plural] You through an example, perhaps: beech, oak, fir, birch have tree as common character. Tree is the species of the named kinds of trees. Individual cases fall respectively again under these individual kinds, this particular fir, beech, and so on. And the self is thus the general species of the subordinate kinds of the I, You, We, [plural] You. To these kinds are again subordinate: this determinate I, this and that determinate You, etc. I, the I whom I myself mean, who says "I," am a case of the kind: I in general. This kind of I falls under the species of the self. Therefore, I am a self.

But the problem with this kind of thinking can be now recognized in the fact that precisely, if I mean myself, I do not necessarily have to say "I," but can and must also say "we." I can take myself in an essential belongingness to the others. In the same fashion, I can be as You. As I, I fall not only under the kind of the I, but also of the You, [plural] You, We. An assignment to a determinate kind, comparable to the beech, oak, birch, is not possible here. There is here a completely different relationship and, with that, no analogy. Though at first it appears that way, the self is not the species. I and You, We and [plural] You are no kinds, the individual I no cases. To be sure, we can, like we just have, lay out the things in words in this manner and move and find our way about in a word-world. It is, however, *empty*. As long as we think as little as possible and the little as indeterminately as possible, we can proceed in this manner. This conceptual order is applicable, however, only to living beings, plants, animals, also to mere things.

But the human being was just defined as rational living being!—But is not the determination of the human being as rational living being a conceptual mistake that does not at all hit on the essence of the human being?

We could now even suppose that the difficulty lies in the fact that we have not yet adequately determined the highest concept of the self analogous to how we can determine trees closer, if we distinguish in them leaves, branches, fruits, and so on, respectively, from other leaves, branches, fruits, and so on. Perhaps we could indeed, if we had a sufficiently distinct concept of the self, derive I and We and You and [plural] You. Why then do we not give any definition of the self? Why do we hesitate?—Because, already with the attempt to define the self and its essence, we force it into a conceptuality and logic that is absolutely foreign to it. Definitions are perhaps applicable to houses, plants, and so on, but not to the human being. For, according to this logic, I, as self, would have to be, after all, an example of the I and, at the same time, also be the other kind (You), which is nonsensical.

This in itself familiar logic of species, kind and cases, this logic, which appears to us as absolutely valid, arose from a definitive experience, from a definitive conception of a kind of beings—a definitive logic beginning in Greek philosophy, under whose rule we still stand today. It seems hopeless to break it; nonetheless, it must happen. Even if we could in the end comprehend the essence of the self, like the essence of a tree, supposing, therefore, that we could accomplish a certain assignment of the I as self and of the You as self—with all such conceptual investigations and classifications, we would have again deviated from the question.

We forget that the What-question returns to us, that we henceforth stand in the realm of the disclosure of the question and that we may not set away from us that about which we are asking, that which is asked about, as a *self in itself*—even if it is finally nevertheless necessary that we execute some sort of objectification, if we ask about the human being in the sense of the questioning-concerning-us-ourselves. Only in this manner is a questioning concerning the human being possible, for only so is an objective, that is, valid answer possible.

In what preceded, we rejected the orientation toward the human being in the direction toward the I, the subject and subjectivity. Yet, is there then an overcoming of the one-sided I-emphasis, if we reduce the question concerning the self to the formula "Who are we ourselves?"? Is that not rather a gross exaggeration of the orientation toward the I? After all, with regard to the question concerning the I in philosophy, one has hitherto left out of account precisely the individual actual I, has asked about the I in general, consciousness in general, [has] wanted to get away precisely from the individual. We, however, must ask about *ourselves*, about our *own* essence. Does that not mean to push egoism, selfishness to extremes? With the question "Who are we ourselves?" we make ourselves after all, as it were, the center of the entire, of the actual and possible humanity! We can already see with this that the reply to the question "What is the human being?" must turn out to be one-sided in the highest degree. The result, therefore, cannot be any that is generally valid and must, therefore, also be scientifically worthless.

These scruples are reasonable, they are even correct under the presupposition of seeing the true answer in the scientific answer. However, this presupposition is not yet decided as legitimate at all. It is perhaps arbitrariness and error, insofar as the questioning concerning the essence in general and in particular the questioning concerning the essence of the human being is no scientific, but a philosophical questioning.

We arrive now in an age in which the question concerning the essence of the human being must be for the first time posed anew as question. This will be a lengthy task. The human being moves now in a position on this planet, with regard to which it is not a matter of indifference who poses the question of who the human being is, and actually, that is, effectively, answers. This question is not of the kind that it springs only as a clever sudden idea from the astuteness of an individual, but behind it and before it stand overpowering necessities. Even these do not always work, so that even the event of the World War in no way has touched on or furthered the question concerning the human being. Victors and vanquished, for the time being, have fallen back into their old condition. Hence, the World War as historical power has not at all yet been won, [has] not yet decided, for the future of our planet. It will not be decided by the question of who has triumphed, but it will be decided by the trial, which the *Völker* are facing. The decision is reached, however, through the answer, which we give to the question of who are we, that is, through our being.

The truth of the answer depends upon the preceding truth of the question. However egoistic the question "Who are we ourselves?" may look in relation to the question "What is the human being?"—Perhaps precisely this kind of questioning could strike down all egoism and all subjectivity, but also conversely rouse up the questioners out of their indifference and detachment. Therefore, we may not rest, but must continuously strive for the right asking of this question.

Recapitulation

We have emphasized a double [point] in the previous lesson: For once, we have shown that the We and the [plural] You are no mere plurality, and secondly, that the self that befits the I, You, We, [plural] You is not characterized by the mere generality of a species that hovers over them.

We can clarify the first state of affairs for ourselves with any number of examples. The [plural] You, in this case, of our own present situation, is given through a peculiar relationship, which is established by the lecture. Besides, it is not the number that is decisive, but a certain selfhood, the unity of the audience. Another example: A company leader at the front lets his company line up and says that at night a dangerous reconnaissance has to be carried out. Volunteers are to report. 20 raise their hands. Of these, he picks out: 1, 2, 3, 4, and so on; he sorts out mere numbers. These 20 have to line up to receive the more detailed command. This We is now, if they line up again, a completely different We, a We who will not be talked about. They are thus as indeterminate, as only something can be; they must take off the last badges so as not to be recognized, they are joined together as those who perhaps will not survive the next day. At the moment of the count by the leader, this We is closed. The number, as manifest as it seems, is here powerless, though it is in a certain sense a necessary determination. Language displays the higher wisdom, by using the [plural] You, not as plural, but in a completely different manner.

We see likewise that also the most superficial form of a collection of any arbitrary number of human beings still has the character of the self and that, precisely through the emphasis on the I, the original unity is split up. Thus, self-being takes a peculiar precedence over the We, You, I and [plural] You.

We tried to make this relationship plain to ourselves, by calling upon known logical relations for help, namely, species, kind, individual case. We did not, however, get through in this manner. Insofar as the single case as such was at the same time an I and You, We and [plural] You, thus falling under several kinds, it became evident that we cannot apply this logical relationship. We cannot grasp the self as species, even if it has the appearance that it stands over the individual.

We had now already strayed again and occupied ourselves prematurely with this, what the self is, instead of persevering in the question "Who are we ourselves?" Here came the objection: Egoism would have to be avoided with the questioning concerning the human being. To what extent the question "Who are we ourselves?" is an egoistic one, cannot be settled beforehand through a theoretical decision. This must show itself from the course of the questioning.

§ 12. The self and self-forlornness

a) The mis-questioning—conditioned by the
    self-forlornness of human being

If we look back to the previous course of our questioning, we notice a constant inclination to question wrongly, to pervert the question. We have not interpolated this mis-questioning artificially, but it lies in the course of this questioning, for which we can also furnish proof from the history of the question concerning the essence of the human being. Behind this mis-questioning stands a definitive necessity, a certain tendency of the human being to stray from the Who-question with this question. We do not hold on tightly to the question by nature precisely because at bottom we do not want to keep to the course of question.

This hidden and unconscious resistance has its ground in the fact that we are first and foremost not with ourselves, roaming about in self-forlornness and self-forgottenness. For this reason, the question concerning the self is unfamiliar, troublesome, uncanny to us. The manner in which the human being asks about the human being depends on how and who he himself is. Conversely, the question of who we are, belongs itself to our being.

The asking of the question "Who are we ourselves?" changes our former being, not in the manner that we add a further question to the previous questions, but that either we ourselves become questionable to ourselves or do not let ourselves be disturbed through this question. This attitude as well alters us, insofar as we now expressly leave it at that, in that we, therefore, do not ask the question or only act as if. The question thus has the peculiarity that we cannot pass by it, but we must go through this question, and we pass through it and out of it somehow inexorably altered. Either we become worthy of question to ourselves, or we pass through it questionless, by closing our mind to it. The question thus has an entirely peculiar character.

We said that the manner in which the question is posed and how we avoid it has its ground in the essence of the human being, in his self-forlornness. Previously, however, we established that a self belongs to the essence of the human being. What about the self-forlornness?

The self-forlornness as well has a definitive relationship with the self—just as the propertyless and the disinherited have a relationship with property and inheritance, what is more, a very sharp one, insofar as they want to snatch up or destroy property. The self is not set away; it is in relation to the self, even in the forlornness. It evades, represses it through all kinds of machinations. Each one of us, none excluded, is constantly in this danger. If one, for example, does not have the desire and the strength to bring the university education to an orderly end, but, on the other hand, finds the sojourn at the university quite pleasant and tolerable, he thus procures a post at the university with the student body. That turns out to be quite entertaining in the era of the political university; he becomes leader of the student body; that is then "political service." In truth, it is an escape from oneself. A thing like that can happen to anyone. That can be so, that must not be so. [Stomping.] [Trans.: The previous brackets appear in the original text.]

A second example—here you can also stomp: A man of average intelligence, lazy, obstinate, must join the SA. Life in the community is, however, disagreeable to him, and it disturbs his nerves. Now he has to take up a theme in the seminar. He finds the work on the theme so important, and the preparations must be so extensive, that he must ask for leave from the SA-Service. This does not happen out of a passion for the science, but it is fundamentally a shirking.

In both cases, selfishness and forlornness are present, and yet a protection of the own self is involved. Those are examples to show us that even the seeming dedication to a task, the self-forgottenness, holds in itself, a relationship with the self.

This self-forlornness is the ground of the difficulty of the actual questioning concerning the self. The self is neither predominantly associated with the I, nor with the You, [plural] You, We. From this, the difficulty arises, where should the self be sought, if it befits neither the We, nor the You or I and [plural] You.

b) Does a preeminence of the We lie in the question
    "Who are we ourselves?"

We asked nevertheless, "Who are *we* ourselves?" With this, we avoided the equation of I and self. At the same time, we have, in addition, the advantage that the question of who *we* ourselves are is timely, as distinguished from the time of liberalism, the I-time. Now is We-time. That might be right, and yet it is trivial, [it] is ambiguous and on the surface, for we can indeed be any beings [who have] come together because of any dubious reasons. "We!"—in this manner, also any nameless crowd speaks. "We!"—in this manner cries also the revolting mass, also the bowling team brags. "We!"—in this manner also a band of robbers arranges to meet. The We alone will not do. Just as the I can constrain and close off the actual self, just as surely can also a We disperse the self-being, turn into herds, incite and even drive to crime.

With the cry "We!" we can miss our self in the same way as in a glorification of the I. Conversely, we can, however, also just as properly find our self-being by way of the I as by way of the [plural] You and We; for all that, it is a matter of the self-being, of the determination of the self. That means: The We, at which we now stop with the question "Who are we ourselves?" the We, also in the sense of genuine community, does not have the preeminence simply and unconditionally, and that also in relation to the community. There are things that are essential and decisive for a community, and precisely these things do not arise in the community, but in the disciplined strength and solitude of an individual. One believes [that] the community is responsible for it; one believes [that] if ten or thirty unprepared and ignorant people squat

together and babble day after day, then a community or a genuine relation results. This camp delusion is the counter-appearance of any camp.

Neither does the We take precedence before the I, nor, conversely,
the I before the We without further ado—as long as in this case the task
is not grasped and posed for wise human beings. The future development will still place us before unusual tasks and compel us to find the
genuine inner limit of a community. There are things that are decisive
for a camp, but precisely that which is essential does not grow in the
camp and out of the camp, but beforehand.

Thus, the We has a fullness of mysteries in itself, which we can
exhaust only with difficulty and which we cannot at all grasp, if we
take the We only as plurality. If, therefore, we pose the question concerning the essence of the human being in the form of the Who and the
Who-question further in the form of the We, then nothing is decided yet
about the self-determination of the self.

We ask again: "Who are we ourselves?"—Whither has the question
brought us?

1. The questioning is of a kind such that an inescapable taking
direction toward ourselves can be experienced in it. Whether we
place ourselves against the question or with it, or whether we let it
pass by in undisturbed placidness—each time, a decision is made
about ourselves. Even if we let the question pass by, we are affected
and branded as those who shirk, those who, however, otherwise continue to do well.

Such questioning after all does not unburden us; it, on the contrary,
adds weight on us, so that the *Dasein* perhaps becomes more weighty,
has a greater draught, must go slower and with greater resistance,
demands greater vigor. With such demands, we do not perhaps become
weaker, but become stronger one day. Whatever our position on the
question, it strikes us one way or another.

2. Next to this taking direction toward ourselves, the questioning is
of such a kind that, depending on who we are ourselves, the question
becomes more capable of being asked or less capable of being asked.
This changing capability of being asked does not mean, however, that
the question would become more familiar to us. For, the more familiar
it is, the less is it genuinely asked. Thus, we have indeed succeeded at
first in aligning the question toward ourselves; yet, we have with this in

no way released the force that is bound in the question. We follow the question concerning ourselves. We know after all [that] the self could remain in self-forlornness. The fact that we are certain of the I-Myself—this certainty proves nothing at all yet.

Even threatened incessantly and in most cases dominated by the self-forlornness—are we we ourselves or with ourselves? Or are we deranged [*ver-rückt*]? That means: moved out [*herausgerückt*] of the track of destination. Have we come into emptiness despite the reeling fullness? Are we still truly beset by the essence of things or are we occupied only with a great variety of things [Trans.: reading *Vielerei* instead of *vielerei*], so that we just barely escape the immense boredom? Are we we ourselves, are we so very alienated from this self that the own self seems strange to us?

It seems to be that way. How else should we have such a long familiar concept of the self, namely, that concept of the self, according to which the self is that which we win through reflexion, through turning around and turning back. Already this common conception of reflexion can divulge that we must seek out again our self out of a turning away, as it were, that the self is that to which we must turn back to again, turn around to. The commonness of this rendering of the self does not yet guarantee its truth, it attests to only one thing: that even out of the alienation, a, if only empty, concept of the self, is created.

And, what is the significance of the demand [that] we should step out of reflectiveness and act unreflectively?—It is not at all proven with this that in this manner the genuine path to the true self is pointed out.

In this way, we sense more and more the questionability lying in the question itself. It becomes questionable:

1. whether we are we ourselves without further ado,
2. whether in general the familiar concept and the usual conception of the self (as what is attainable in the reflexion) has arisen from the proper self and is able to point out to us the proper path; for, this concept could also be a sign of self-forlornness.
3. finally, it is questionable, out of which direction, from where, shall we take the answer to the question concerning the Who, which character the answer shall have. For, in the course of the questioning we direct ourselves to the realm out of which the answer shall come to us.

Does it not seem as if the question is through and through question-able, that it is not worthwhile to ask [*verlohnt*]? Because, if there is nothing on which we stand, then we also can no longer take any question-step.

c) Outer and inner identification of the We

We have not yet fixed our eyes on one thing, namely, the We, that is, those who we ourselves are. We have, to be sure, shown that the concept "We" is not to be conceived as plural. We have understood that the We is *we ourselves* and that we address and pronounce ourselves in this question.

The community of individual human beings lets itself in fact be determined distinctly, perhaps by specifying the geographical place on the planet, which is indeed a distinct one: One could even consult the location of the planet itself in its path in the solar system and outer space. At the same time, the point in time can be unequivocally deter-mined, the position in the numerical series of the years up to the day and hour. We ourselves are uniquely and in an unrepeatable manner determined through this specification of the here and now. However, are *we* determined by this?

These specifications, as important as they may be, have the same inalterable possibility of determination; they attune and determine in the same manner, if instead of humans, we put just as many dogs or cats or stones. We are in no manner determined through these specifica-tions, which are correct.

One will say that those are precisely external characterizations of place and time; we must start with the inner core. We could now arrange the individual courses of life, equip them with characterologi-cal expert opinions, perhaps even complemented with skull measure-ments, and so on. We will miss ourselves with this just as much as with the geographical-astronomical assumptions. Even if we filed all results completely in catalogues and registered them in curves, this declaration and determination of ourselves, despite the many considerations, would be a ridiculous effort.

It is not that simple to pose the form of the determination for our-selves in an adequate sense—not as if we ourselves were in an entire-ly extraordinary manner difficult to determine, but because we see wrongly out of sheer zeal, because we believe that here it is about findings and descriptions, [that] it is about the fact that we are addressed, instead of about those who pronounce *themselves, they themselves* in the *We.*

Recapitulation

Our question "Who are we ourselves?" is grounded in the respective manner of our self-being. For this reason, it is possible that we unknowingly or knowingly resist this question, [that we] evade it—assuming that we move in a self-forlornness and want to hold on to this: in a self-forlornness, which is not a setting-away of the self, but encloses a definitive comportment toward the self. The human being remains also in the self-forlornness with himself and with his essence, only he has now *fallen* into the unessence of his essence.

The evasion of the question lies all the nearer because it has the peculiarity of not letting anyone who steps in its circumference pass by it untouched. Each must decide in the face of this question whether he takes over the question or whether he perseveres in questionlessness or whether he—indifferently—tries to push the question away from himself. In favor of the fact that the self-forlornness belongs to the actual essence of the self, stands, as infallible evidence, that the conception of the self that has been common for centuries is attained precisely from self-forlornness—insofar as we determine the self here as that which we can reach in the *retrogression*, in the *reflexion*, as if the human being had departed from himself and had to carry out a turning around to himself.

If the self-being is questionable, then we too, who pose the question, cannot simply go straight ahead and question who we ourselves are—without having secured whether and how we ourselves are in general. And this, without circumscribing the We, cannot be answered in more detail. Even the We-form prejudges no definite answer, in the manner perhaps in which the We would have precedence before the You and I.

Even where a genuine community entirely determines the self-being, this is not in every respect that which is decisive, that which is essential for the community. In many regards, that which is decisive is never attained in and out of the community, but out of the disciplined strength of an individual in his solitude, who evidently must have in himself the impetus that entitles him to the solitude.

In the task of circumscribing the We, we tried first the way from outside, by determining the geographical place and the astronomical time.

We saw, however, immediately that this kind of determination holds for any kind of beings that we substitute for ours. Just as little as a geographical-astronomical determination can an inner characteristic arranged by us, perhaps grounded biologically or on courses of life, touch on our *Dasein* here and now.

§ 13. "'We' are the Volk" by virtue of decision

Thus, the question arises: How do we carry out this determination? We, who we are now here, as we bluntly pronounce our present and local *Dasein*, are involved in the happening of education of a school, which ought to be the University of Academic Education. We subordinate ourselves to the demands of this education, prepare ourselves for vocations, whose practice is grounded in a knowledge characteristic of each. We set our wills in advance in these vocations, which serve as such, be it education, be it the strengthening and training, be it the inner order of the *Volk,* and so on.

As we are fitted [*eingefügt*] in these demands of the University, we will the will of a State, which itself wills to be nothing else than the sovereign will of the government and the form of government of a *Volk* over itself. We as *Dasein* submit ourselves [*fügen uns*] in a peculiar manner into the membership of the *Volk*, we stand in the being of the *Volk*, we are this *Volk* itself.

As we thus pronounce ourselves, that is, speak with one another, we have carried out an entirely different determination of the *Volk* than hitherto, we have now also completely unawares answered the question "Who are we ourselves?": We stand in the being of the *Volk*, our self-being is the *Volk*. Unawares, we have answered, without roaming out in cosmic spaces and times, without engaging in the motives of our state of mind.

What happened? We submitted ourselves [*fügten uns*] to the *moment*. With the phrase "We are here," involved in a happening of education, something is carried out. According to the wording, it appears admittedly as if we had accomplished a description of what takes place here —only in another line of sight. Yet, this is not the case. We can examine it, by investigating whether we could say in saying together [*in Mitsprache*] what was just pronounced: "Yes, I will it so. I will to subordinate myself to the demands, to submit myself to the power of a will, to stand together with wills [*mit Willen mitstehn*]." We could examine ourselves, whether we will that or whether we would say "no" or whether we had to confess that we carried out neither the Yes nor the No, but have only come here and let ourselves drift along [*mittreiben*].

We have carried out no description. This "We are here" does not mean a plurality of human beings is present-at-hand, but "We are here! We are ready! Let it happen!"

We are thus through a sequence of decisions, whether one way or another, [we] are decided or undecided. Some decisiveness now constitutes our self. The small and narrow We of the moment of the lecture has transposed us at once into the *Volk*, better: [it has] made clear to us that and how we are transposed into the *Volk*. It is necessary, therefore, instead of lengthy descriptions, to take up our moment, in order to submit ourselves only to it so that we discover ourselves in it. A *reflexion* at the same time is not required.

We see distinctly that all that has nothing to do with science. We need here no *facts*, nor do we ascertain anything whatever in its particular present-at-hand being. It does not let itself be proven in an objective sense whether we have spoken together [*mitgesprochen*] from out of the moment, [whether we] have gone through the decision, whether we are let into the happening. The talk sounds like an observation, perhaps this: The fields are too dry in these rainless weeks. Moreover, the talk can even be mere empty talk, which we have talked along [*mitgeredet*] without thinking, also without willing. Or instead we said, "We are there, we are involved" actually out of and from within ourselves and in the manner of engaging ourselves in the moment.

No individual person among you can in any manner ascertain about any individual person how he has decided. You, as well, cannot say how I myself have held my lecture, whether after the manner of decision or only in the manner of reporting or as phrase. Correspondingly, we ourselves are *we*, in each case according to *how* we are, in the similarity and sameness of the wording. We are *properly* we only in the decision, namely, each one singly.

It seems as if now the individuals must be pushed together into the plurality only afterwards. However, that is not so. The decision does not move the individual back up to the I, but broadens him toward self-*Dasein* in education. In willing to be he himself, he is sent out precisely beyond himself into the belongingness to which he submits himself in the decision. In the decision, each is separated from each in such a way *as only* a human being can be separated. That is so in any decision, even in a decision that concerns solely a community, for example, the forging of a friendship. This decision as well distances those who have decided as far as only a distance can possibly be. Such relations are not in any case grounded in external nearness, so that those who are dependent, who snuggle up to another, would be those suitable for friendship. Friendship grows only out of the greatest possible inner independence of each individual, which is evidently something completely different from egoism. In spite of the separation after the manner of decision of the individual, a concealed *unison* carries itself out here, whose concealedness is an essential one. This unison is fundamentally always a mystery.

Where do we stand now in our questioning? —We saw that now also the We, which we believed we could describe, determines itself only in the decision. Now we see that the We is more than something that is merely nugatory: the We is no pushing together of persons into a mere sum, the We is a decision-like one. *How* the We is, respectively, is dependent upon our decision, assuming that we decide.

At the moment in which we have grasped the we as decision-like, the decision about our self-being has also been reached. A decision was already reached, who we ourselves are, namely, the Volk.

We have, however, become more keen of hearing and more attentive in the course of our investigations, and thus also here reservations mount in us; we could have already again come off the track and have turned off the course.

Who are we ourselves? Answer: the *Volk*. We have to register to this answer a series of reservations and doubts.

1. This answer seems to have been attained rather hastily and, therefore, superficially, given out of the momentary reflection and attained without closer grounding.
2. The answer appears to be incorrect, for we, the few, surely cannot be equated with the *Volk*. It shows, if not presumption, nevertheless, lack of a necessary distinction.

3. If already our self-being is brought into connection with the *Volk*, then it should at first be said: We are a *Volk*, not the *Volk*.

These three thoughts obviously converge into a difficulty: that we, namely, here have spoken about something, without saying what we mean with it. The question thus arises: What is that, a *Volk*?

Still something else makes understanding difficult. We said, the We is a We that is after the manner of decision. Now, however, it is precisely not placed in our will whether we belong to the *Volk* or not; that, to be sure, cannot be decided through our passing of a resolution. For, that is always already decided, without our willing, based on our descent, about which we ourselves have not decided. Citizenship, one can perhaps will, but belongingness to a *Volk* never. What is the purpose, therefore, of a decision here?

Two essential interposed questions, therefore, arise here:

1. What is a *Volk*?
2. What does decision mean?

We will see that both questions are interconnected.

In the continuation of our guiding question "Who are we ourselves?" we now, therefore, make a pause that is necessary for answering the interposed questions.

§14. Reply to the first interposed question:
What is that, a Volk?

The first question can be set in motion in different ways. We intentionally take an external point of departure, namely, with the word "*Volk*." We are briefly pursuing the fact that the word "*Volk*" diverges into a manifold of meanings; for this, we give examples of the most common word usage. In the review of the word "*Volk*," however, we remain conscious of the fact that, through the gathering together of the word meanings and the extraction of an average meaning, we are not able to grasp the essence of the *Volk*.

We listen to *Volk* songs and see *Volk* dances, visit a *Volk* festival. We take part in delivering the lists to the households with the purpose of the census [*Volkszählung*]. Measures are taken for increasing and securing public health [*Volksgesundheit*]. The racial movement [*völkische Bewegung*] wants to bring the *Volk* back to the purity of their racial breed.

Frederick the Great calls the *Volk* an animal with many tongues and few eyes. On November 12, 1933, the *Volk* was polled. A police chief commands: "Disperse the *Volk* with clubs!" On August 1, 1914, the *Volk* stood in arms. Of the German *Volk,* 18 million dwell outside of the State's borders. Karl Marx calls "*Volk*" the totality of workers as distinguished from the loafers and exploiters. The spirit of the *Volk* is in romanticism the ground root for faith, poetry, and philosophy. Religion is opium for the *Volk.*

What does "*Volk*" mean in all of these expressions? If one talks about the polling of the *Volk* and, if the police disperses the *Volk*, does "*Volk*" then mean the same?

In the polling of the *Volk* on November 12, 1933, the *Volk* as a whole was polled. Of course, only those entitled to vote were polled. Do not the others, minors, belong to the *Volk*? Do we mean only the countable sum of entitled voters on the lists?

In a census of the *Volk*, is the *Volk* counted whose *Volk* songs we listen to? Or is the *Volk* of *Volk* art in general not numerable, so that in the first case we count only the population? Does the moment lie in the *Volk* spirit of romanticism, which also belongs to the *Volk*, which shall be kept healthy? Does public health [*Volksgesundheit*] concern the *Volk* in Karl Marx's sense, or do the bourgeois also belong to it? Is the *Volk* in arms the *Volk* whom Frederick the Great named the animal with many tongues and few eyes?

We detect at once here definitive differences, but still without instantly being able to grasp adequately the character of these differences. Yet, as far as the meanings also may diverge, just as certainly do we nevertheless sense in a blur a concealed unity.

It suggests itself now to line up the different concepts according to the rules of the ancient logic in order to select what is common to all. Thus, we arrive at an entirely empty representation: *Volk* as human unit or *Volk* as living being or organism.

However, why do we not leave to the word its ambiguity? Is it really necessary to force everything into the straightjacket of concepts? We understand after all what is meant by "*Volk*." Certainly, that can suffice, perhaps for the claims of an understanding at the level of a quick newspaper reader. If this level is supposed to be decisive and standard, then we could break off our considerations. If this common and, within certain limits, legitimate kind of understanding, however, is not enough, what then ought to happen?

In no way do we want to aspire to and advocate for a law for the standardization of language, but we want to understand that here an inner multifold of beings appears. This one, named "*Volk*," forces us to experience and to interpret it according to different respects. This scatteredness is the sign of the concealed fullness of the essence, but also of the manifoldness of its unessence. All the more rigorously must we see to it to hit on the questioned unity adequately.

Instead of logically seeing the manifoldness of word meanings together and, with this, look at concepts, a preparatory step shall be taken now in such a manner that we try to look at the being meant by the word and bring out the lines of sight that manifest themselves in the different word meanings. We do not, however, want to leave it at these different lines of sight; rather, we want to try to see how these different lines of sight after all provide a certain unity of that which belongs together in the word "*Volk*."

Thus, the danger of a merely conceptual dismemberment does not exist. In order for us not to get confused on this way, [that is, not] to get confused through the disintegration of the matter into word meanings, we will have to speak in a proving and understanding fashion from immediate experience.

Recapitulation

We had prepared the question "Who are we ourselves?" thus far so that we could try to procure an answer for ourselves. The first step was that we sought to determine the We closer:

1. through a place- and time-determination,
2. through the attempt at a presentation of that which is "biological."

We came on this way, however, only to see the We, in a manner of speaking, from outside—as an assembly of individual human beings.

We tried then another way, namely, from out of the moment. We said: We are *here*, admitted into the happening of education of this university and, with this, fitted into the vocation, which we willed with its professional tasks, [and] with this, fitted into the order and the willing of a State. We are *here*, fitted into this happening today, we are *here* in the belongingness to this Volk, we are this *Volk* itself.

This sounds like a descriptive observation of ourselves, nevertheless, it has another character. The joint-execution of this situation is a succession of decisions, through which we go here, a succession, which each individual carries out for himself, so that none of us can ascertain with regard to the other whether the decision is carried out. Though we separate ourselves in the decision, we are not in this decision pressed back to ourselves in the sense of egoism; through this decision, we are rather sent out beyond ourselves and sent into the membership of the *Volk*. In this situation, a concealed unison of ourselves arises so that we in fact could say "we."

The result "We are the *Volk*" is subject to essential doubts now. One can say that we have proceeded too hastily with this question, that we have taken a leap, namely, from ourselves to the whole of the *Volk*. All those who we are here, the few, claim to be the *Volk*. And finally, we would have to say, of course: not the *Volk*, but a *Volk*.

All of that cannot be decided as long as it remains undetermined what "*Volk*" means. In this way, we came before the question: "What does '*Volk*' mean?" Since thus the membership of the *Volk* is decision-like, a further question is connected with this: "What does decision mean here?"

We have tackled the clarification of the first question. We started with an external enumeration of the different concepts of *Volk*. "*Volk*" in the sense of the *Volk* song, of *Volk* festival, of *Volk* way, of the census, polling of the *Volk*, "*Volk*" in the meaning: the *Volk* is dispersed from one another; *Volk* in arms, "*Volk*" as animal with many tongues and few eyes, "*Volk*" in the sense of that which is to be brought back to its peculiar nature; "*Volk*"—idealized in romanticism (spirit of the *Volk*); "*Volk*" as totality of the working population (Marx); "*Volk*" in the phrase: Religion is opium for the *Volk*.

The task now is not for us to distill out general concepts in the sense of the old logic, but the course of question, in which what is here addressed each time respectively with "*Volk*" is meant, is to be highlighted. We must see whether within the different lines of sight a peculiar unity is to be grasped, on the ground of which we can speak about "*Volk*" in a manifold meaning.

a) *Volk* as body

In a census, the *Volk* is counted in the sense of the population, the population, insofar as it constitutes the body of the *Volk*, the inhabitants of a land. At the same time, it is to be considered that in a governmental order of the census a certain part of the *Volk* is included, namely, the part that dwells within the State's borders. The German nationals living abroad are not included in the count, [they] do not belong in this sense to the *Volk*. On the other hand, those can also be included in the count, those who, taken racially, are of alien breed, do not belong to the *Volk*.

Census is, therefore, only a census of residents. The population politics, however, does not mean the residents; it means the vital relations like the family, whose health is to be looked after. Here, population is taken in a definitive sense, as body of the *Volk* in the sense of the corporeal life.

Often, we use the word "*Volk*" also in the sense of "race" (for example, also in the phrase "racial movement"). What we name "race" has a relation to the corporeal, bloodline connection of the members of the *Volk*, their lineages. The word and the concept "race" is no less ambiguous than "*Volk*." That is no accident, since both are connected.

"Race" ["*Rasse*"] means not only that which is racial as the bloodline in the sense of heredity, of hereditary blood connection and of the drive to live, but means, at the same time, often that which is racy [*das Rassige*]. This is not, however, confined to corporeal qualities, but we say, for example, also "snazzy [*rassiges*] car" (at least the young boys). That which is racy embodies a certain rank, provides certain laws, does not concern in the first place the corporeality of the family and of the lineage. Racial in the first sense does not by a long shot need to be snazzy, it can rather be very drab.

"*Volk*" was now, therefore, at first understood as population, residents, connection of lineages—the *Volk* as <u>body of the Volk</u>.

b) *Volk* as soul

In the folk songs, folk festivals and folk customs, the emotional life of the *Volk* shows itself, the allegorical form of the fundamental bearing of its *Dasein*. The *Volk* is here no longer an arbitrary population and residents, but a certain vicinity of human beings, adapted to grown settlements. It is not established in an arbitrary, unrelated region, but with the settlement, the *Volk* first of all constitutes itself with its customs, it gives the land also its characteristics, for example, through the use of the water power, and so on; and even the animal- and plant-world are also molded by the settlement, if also often in the negative sense of extermination. Conversely, the thus molded landscape juts out into the day-by-day of the communitary *Dasein* in the alternation of its temporal events of birth, marriage, death, and change of seasons.

"*Volk*" is taken here in their psychical [*seelischen*] conduct—as *soul* [Seele].

c) *Volk* as spirit

However, with the *Volk* as soul we have already a limited region opposite the whole of the population that is registered in a census. The many in the rear buildings of the large city, for whom weather does not even exist, also belong to the population; to it also belong, however, the many who do not at all count themselves among the *Volk*, who take the *Volk* with custom and practices only as an element, as object of pleasure on a summer vacation.

Here, it turns out that this confined concept of "*Volk*" also implies the meaning of a peculiar stratification: *Volk* is here a determinate lower stratum, which, however, at the same time, also on its own initiative wants to persevere in that which is impulsive, often also in that which is unrestrained. The *Volk* in the latter sense is understood from the *Volk*, insofar as it is taken socially. A *Volk* as lower stratum belongs to the human society next to the proper one, the so-called better society.

We have, therefore, two meanings that intersect: on the one hand, a whole of the *Volk* (like Romanic and Germanic *Völker*), on the other hand, a separation into *Volk* (rabble) and better society. This separation into social strata occurs not only in a property society or in an economic society, but is also possible in a class society. The separation of a *Volk* can, in turn, come about out of standards and points of view, which can be taken from the global culture. And the decision power of a *Volk* shall bring it back to its own law.

In all of this, where it is about classification, autonomous order, decision, *Volk* is as historical, after the manner of knowing, as according to willing, spiritual: *Volk* as *spirit*.

In sum, we have highlighted three respects under which the concept "*Volk*" stands:

1. Volk as body [Körper / Leib],
2. *Volk* as soul,
3. *Volk* as spirit.

Body, soul, spirit are, however, components of the human being. To be sure, in the ruling definition, the human being is determined precisely with regard to body, soul, spirit. The *Volk* is thus taken as human being on a large scale, as it were.

Where do we stand now with our answer? To the question "Who are we ourselves?" we have answered, "We are the *Volk*." The question to which we wanted to respond with this answer reads: "What is the human being?" We had answered to this: "The human being is the *Volk*," but that is: The *Volk* is the human being on a large scale.

That is no answer, for

1. we answer with that which we asked about;
2. with our answer "The *Volk* is the human being on a large scale; it is that which is corporeal, mental, spiritual large," not only are the components of the human being taken up after all, but even transferred to something larger; this transfer makes the components even more indeterminate, more blurred and more worthy of question;
3. the determination of the essence of the human being as an animal equipped with reason, with mental power, takes the human being as something that somehow occurs, that can be described.

However, we already recognized earlier that we miss the human being in his self-being with this. That is why we had earlier transformed the What-question into the Who-question. We wanted to turn our back precisely *to those* representations according to which the human being is taken in the composition of body, soul, spirit. Now, we are turning back again, however, to the same course of question. This answer is dubitable in the highest degree. Perhaps, we cannot at all answer: "We are the *Volk*."

Before we decide to relinquish the answer, however, we must grasp the *Volk* in its essence in a more determinate manner and try to ground these determinations. We could for this purpose follow a new science, sociology, that is, the doctrine of the forms of society and of community. Within sociology, multiple things are said about the concept of the *Volk*, particularly, about the demarcation of society from State and *Reich* and so on.

To be sure, it must here be seen to it whence the definitions are taken and whether they do not deviate into emptiness, whether these determinations are not fundamentally on a wrong track, insofar as concepts like "*Volk*" and "State" in general cannot be defined, but must be comprehended as historical, as belonging, respectively, to an historical being [*Sein*]. On the other hand, we cannot, however, do without a determinate-unitary concept of the *Volk*.

It will depend on replying to the question concerning the essence of the *Volk* in the same style in which we asked in general—thus in *the* course of the question to which the answer "We are the *Volk*" has been given: in the course of the Who-question. Therefore, even here, we may not ask, "What is a *Volk*?" in order to come to a hackneyed definition, but" "What is *this Volk*, which we ourselves are?"

We heard already that the question "What is this *Volk*, which we ourselves are?" is a question of decision. This question sets us before the further question: "Are we, then, this *Volk*, which we ourselves are?" That seems to be an odd question. How shall something that is, precisely not be what it is? It just belongs to the essence of a being that it is that what it is.

But, perhaps this general statement holds only for definitive realms of beings and not for every one. It is presumably senseless to ask about the plant: "Is it that what it is?" The plant cannot in its essence deviate from this essence.

However, what about the being that here stands in question, what about ourselves? Do we not have the unique privilege that we can stray from our essence and become untrue to it, that we can lose ourselves and turn into the unessence of our essence and persevere for long in it? With this, however, the question "Are we the *Volk*, which we ourselves are?" would not at all be as senseless as it appeared at first. The question "Are we the *Volk*, which we ourselves are" is perhaps in the highest measure pressing and unavoidable. Then, however, our self-being is in a strange way: We are then in being [*seiend*] not those who we are.

What, then, do "in being" and "are" mean here? Thus far, we have asked the question "Who are we ourselves?" without restraint, as it were, and believed that with the modification of the What-question into the Who-question the matter would be settled. That we are, is beyond the question. Who would also not know what "Who are we?" means? The cherries are ripe, the weather is muggy. Now, however, it appears: We are those who we are in *that* way that we perhaps are not *we*. This "perhaps" is not addition, but belongs necessarily to it.

This *Are* and *Being* stand under a decision. With the change of the What-question into the Who-question, we are *ourselves*, not only the interrogative, changed. The whole sense of the questioning has become another one, not only the We is after the manner of decision, but also the being [*das Sein*]. Hence the second inquiry of doubt: "What does decision mean here?" It must be posed because otherwise the answer "We are the *Volk*" remains incomprehensible too.

To all appearances, the membership in the *Volk* does not stand in the realm of a decision, but it is always already decided about. We do not at all know, however, what "decision" shall mean here first of all; consequently, we do not know what [this] shall mean: The *Volk* has the character of decision. We have, however, seen that being can be changed into nonbeing, without thereby sinking into the nothing, that we, therefore, are not in being [*nichtseiend*], yet are.

§ 15. Reply to the second interposed question: What does decision mean?

We are, therefore, taking up the question "What does decision mean?" and dropping the question "What is a *Volk*?" for the time being. We have now experienced the ambiguity and one-sidedness of the orientation toward the human being and his states, and have grasped the question "Who is this *Volk*?" as question of decision. "Who is this *Volk*?" is a question that first gains clarity as question of decision, if we know about decision as such.

In the regulations for the execution of a competition, it is said with regard to the awarding of the competition prize: By equal achievements, the lot decides. Depending on how the lot falls (with the coin, whether the image is visible or covered), it can be read off to whom the prize shall be delivered. The fall of the lot eliminates the one, and the prize is assigned to the other. However, strictly speaking, no decision making takes place here in the process of the draw, because the lot cannot at all decide, assuming that we understand by decision [*Entscheidung*] at the same time a choosing between possibilities. In the case of the draw, a separation [*Scheidung*] of one from the other, an *elimination* [Ausscheidung] is brought about by accident. There is a separating between [*geschieden zwischen*] , but there is no deciding about [*entschieden über*] .

The matter stands differently, if the regulations read, "Given equal achievements, the umpire decides." Here, there is decision, and, to be sure, not because it is, at the same time, decided about the one and the other in this or that way—insofar as the umpire has both before himself, knows their achievements—but a decision is present here, because now the separation and elimination can only happen insofar as the umpire *himself* decides, and that means, sets himself for one against the other.

The lot merely falls; it does not decide in the above discussed sense. This falling is indeed only willed in order to avoid a decision. Thus, behind this flight in the face of a decision, there stands, nevertheless, a decision, namely this one: not to decide and to will not to decide.

In the other case, the umpire decides, he himself decides as awarder of the prize. He becomes in this decision he who he should be, he becomes *he himself*. Before this decision, he is not at all this self. He can indeed also, though he makes the decision, evade making a decision, perhaps by saying to himself: "I award the prize to him who stands spatially closest to me." In this case, he decides—and, yet, [this is] only an accident.

We see here: Only the genuine decision turns the judge into he who he should be, not by the fact that he thinks about himself, but conversely by the fact that he entirely disregards his inclinations and moods and prejudices and decides entirely out of that, from where he should decide—without a reflecting comportment, therefore, without egoistic self-centeredness. We see already here the peculiar connection between genuine decision and proper self-being.

For us, the question is now, how do things stand with the decision by saying, "We are involved in the happening of education of this university."

a) Decision and decisiveness

We said, we are involved in the happening of education of this university. We said, this *We* and *Are* is decision-like. A decision in the sense of the self-deciding of each individual is present, but not so that the one decides against or for *the other*, but for or against *himself*. Nonetheless, that is surely not a reflexive decision, but a decision for being-involved or against the same. It is not a matter of decision whether we are here factually present-at-hand, but it is a matter of decision whether we want to act jointly, whether we want to act jointly or contrariwise. This decision is not coming to an end at the moment; it is set, but it begins only then and lasts on, it becomes *decisiveness*.

In the case of the awarding of the prize on the other hand, the matter is finished with the execution of the decision. X receives his prize, and the sportscast announces that the decision is made. The decision, however, which *we* make, is not finished with the execution, but it only just begins. Wherein consists this decision, since we, to be sure, cannot decide into the indeterminate? A decision just in general is always *no* decision; we can always only decide for *this* and *only* for this. We, however, also do not want to philosophize in emptiness, but we ask about the concept only in order to decide.

Wherein does this decision consist? Perhaps in the single act, which I now carry out (or carried out in the previous lesson), by pulling myself together, as it were, clenching the teeth together and, with a hard facial expression, saying, " I am decided"—whereupon everything remains as it was? This "I have decided" is pronounced in the form of the past tense, but it is in essence oriented toward that which occurs and how it occurs, namely, the continuation of the previous happening of education: I have decided to loaf no more, to take my exam, to earn the grades; I will then scrupulously pursue the practical professional training, fill my post and thus become an honest man and a useful member of the community of the *Volk*.

One could plead that a decision of such kind is today no longer necessary or is self-evident, since indeed the student body of 1933 has issued the watchword that the time of the idle student is over. And yet the possibility remains that this well-behaved decisiveness with all its orderliness closes itself off toward the proper happening. One will say, that is indeed today no longer possible. The student of today will affirm and carry out the duties of the SA and of the student organization, and so on.—Has he proven with this that he has engaged in today's happening? In no way. Firstly, one can accomplish all of these services without being touched by the happening. And secondly, it is not at all settled that these institutions are, with all of their inner necessities, capable of actually altering the happening of education of this university. They could remain an incidental, though necessary, means of education—and they will remain that, as long as the university has not altered itself from the new actuality according to its inner law.

One will say: That is happening now after all. One wants to alter the university, perhaps set it in the Allemanic space. Yet, by the fact that one talks about the region of the university, the university does not become different—where not even two percent of teachers and students speak and understand the language of this region.

After all, now one also begins to shorten the lectures, for example, in medicine, from five to three hours. That is perhaps very appropriate. However, with this, it is not guaranteed that the lectures become better, for perhaps the old lectures are only condensed through this. Just as little is it certain that a seminar becomes better, if one lets it take place on a green meadow instead of between four walls.

The rector can appear today in the SA uniform instead of the traditional robe. Has he proven with this that the university itself has changed? At best, it is veiled that at bottom everything remains as it was. We can perfectly adjust ourselves in the new duties and institutions and yet close our minds to the proper happening.

Fundamentally, now one will say, "One has still not at all dealt with the proper task of the university, with the determination of the university as teaching institution." It should not only be taught what serves the prompt training for the occupation, but there should be research; *science* should be promoted. Many believe, therefore, the much-reproved research is the foundation for teaching, and the era starts anew, where he is regarded as perfect student who takes the shape of an unsuccessful university lecturer. Yet, also with this, one can close one's mind to the proper happening. Though one would like to save the merit of the conception that teaching itself should be based on research, because otherwise teaching silts up and deteriorates into a tedious cramming operation. Yet, as correct as this conception seems to be, it, nevertheless, suffers an essential mistake. One can be an extraordinary researcher and yet not be capable of surveying the whole of one's field of knowledge. And a "good teacher" can be merely a skilled crammer.

Here it is neither about research, nor about teaching, but about being beset and seized out of the whole by the essence of things that hold them. Today's discussion is only the sign for the fact that one has not yet comprehended what it is about; it gives evidence that we, even now, are still in the state in which the university hastens toward its end. The disintegration into fields is the end of the university, which for decades has been already there, because for a long time a unitary pedagogical fundamental power is missing. Is there no longer any united creative capacity and self-affirmation of the German *Volk*'s power, but only the being bent on the hitherto?

We deplore, not the dissolution, not the end, but the fact that one veils this end, tries to cover it up in all sorts of ways—precisely on the side of those who revolutionize and do not notice that we are only conserving a corpse, a pseudo-unity.

b) Resoluteness as engagedness of the human being in the happening
   that is forthcoming

What shall be said with all that?—That we decide in favor of the discharge of today's students' obligations, for exams, reform, for the consequences of scientific works—with all of these decisions, we close our minds, instead of opening our minds to the proper happening. These decisions are after all only the affirmation of the hitherto; no self-opening [*Sichöffnen*] happens, no *resoluteness* [Entschlossenheit], but a blind being bent on that which is usual, upon that which is comfortable.

A remarkable situation has arisen: On one side stand those who are worried about procuring for this edifice the largest possible roof with lighting rods; they will lay down the foundation later. On the other side are those who affirm the present, but do not leave the hitherto, taking one step forward and two backwards. On both sides, there is no genuine decision.

It is an error to believe that there would be a reaction at the German university. There is no reaction, because there is no upheaval (revolution) there, and this is not because one has not understood where one shall begin. Certain people also do not want a revolution at all; it could namely turn out that they themselves thereby prove to be highly superfluous.

Thus, there is something remarkable about the decision in which we stand at the moment, for the one who comprehends—a peculiarity, which no longer lets us come out of the restlessness. It does not suffice merely to parrot this, but it is important to comprehend that behind all that an uncanny ambiguity of life and of action can establish itself.

Yet, how shall we carry out the decision differently? Here too, it makes itself felt that we are we ourselves in a certain manner, yet, nevertheless, do not stand *properly* in this being. This is not overcome through speeches, but only through radical reeducation—and [it] will also be overcome.

We grasped our decision in the phrase "We are admitted in the happening of education of the university," [and we] emphasized that this *We* and *Are* is *after the manner of decision*. We expected a clarification of this phrase from a conceptual discussion of that which we call "decision." It turned out that the decision, which we meant there and perhaps carry out, strictly speaking, is no proper decision at all in the sense in which we claim and named it a "resoluteness." It is important to say what we mean by this, or better: it is important *to enter into a resoluteness* or to prepare the possibility for it.

The decision, as we have meant it hitherto, was the execution of an affirmative or negative choice of the today and of the hitherto. This deciding, this decisiveness is a closing of one's mind vis-à-vis the happening, instead of an opening up of this happening. Now, we could perhaps say: Decisiveness and resoluteness are the same. They are only two words for the same thing.—We use, however, the word "resoluteness" based on a new view of the effect. We are decided for something, a decision for this something was made. Nonetheless, we cannot only put off the execution and the consequences of this decision, but, above all, also not attend to the matter further, and on occasion come back to it. The smoker has decided to give up smoking, but wants to begin only next week. He is decided [*entschieden*], but not resolved [*entschlossen*]. It is certain that he is still smoking in three weeks.

We are resolved to something—in this lies the fact that that to which we are resolved stands constantly before us, determining all of our being; it does not occupy us occasionally, but the resoluteness gives our being a definitive form and constancy. It is not meant with this any condition that one carries around with oneself, just as we say: He is a human being capable of deciding. In resoluteness, the human being is rather *engaged* in the *happening that is forthcoming*. Resoluteness is itself an event, which *fore-grasping* that happening, constantly co-determines the happening.

Resoluteness is an event, not in the customary meaning of any occurrence, not any act, but resoluteness has its own constancy in itself, so that I do not at all need to repeat the resolution. If I must repeat the resolution, I prove that I am not yet resolved. Resoluteness is a distinctive event [*Geschehnis*] *in* a happening [*Geschehen*].

Third Chapter

The Question Concerning
the Essence of History

With resoluteness, we stand in the region of history, not in any arbitrary realm of incidents, but in that which we in an emphatic sense call history and now have to deal with.

We are, of course, not presuming now to develop here, let alone to answer, the question concerning the essence of history. On the other hand, it must be said that the question concerning the essence of history is none other than our guiding question: "Who is the human being?" For, only the human being has history, because only he alone can be history insofar as he is and [is] according to the circumstances.

What is history? It seems as if we were going farther and farther away from our theme. We began with the question: "What is language?" This led us to the questions: "What is the human being?"—"Who is the human being?"—"Who is the self?"—"What is *Volk*?"—"What is decision?"— "What is history?" How do we arrive in the process at the theme of logic: "What is the essence of language?"—We are dealing continuously with the essence of language, without it being transparent to us.

The question concerning the essence of history is subject entirely to the same difficulties as the guiding question. For this reason, the question is to be kept in the framework of our discussions. Nonetheless, it is necessary to give a broader overview of the essence of history in order to comprehend what matters to us here.

§16. The determination of the essence of history is grounded in the
     character of history of the respective era. The essence of truth—
     determined by the historical *Dasein*

We dispense with giving a report of the up to now and presently valid
conception of history, or with criticizing it. Rather, we place at the beginning of our discussion the statement: The determination of the essence of
history is grounded in the respective character of history of the era from
which this determination is carried out.

There is no downright binding circumscription of the essence of
history in itself. It makes no sense to apply the medieval conception of
history to our era; just as senseless is it to characterize that conception
of history as false.—However, then there is really no absolute truth! Of
course not. It is time that we cure ourselves of the consternation over
this and finally take seriously that we are for the time being still human
beings and no gods.

From the fact that there is no absolute truth for us, however, we may
not infer that there is in general no truth for us. By truth, we understand
the manifestness of beings, which manifestness fits and binds us into
the being of beings—in each case, according to the kind of being of the
beings that enter here into manifestness. What for us is true in this
sense of truth is quite enough for a human life.

There is no need for any hackneyed truth, which is true for everyone
and, therefore, binding for no one. A truth does not become less of a
truth by the fact that not everyone can appropriate it. However, even if
everyone can agree to a truth, this truth does not need to be true; and
conversely, one individual can stand in the truth, in which others do not
stand, because they are not ripe for that. This truth does not thereby by
chance become false.

But now, what about the following thought: If there is for us, as it is,
no absolute truth, then at least the statement "There is no absolute truth"
must be absolutely true. With this, there is, *nevertheless,* absolute truth,
and the statement "There is no absolute truth" is broken through.

This inference is a small formal piece of art. However, from the
statement "There is no absolute truth," it does not follow that the statement itself is absolutely true; it is true only for us. It is important to put
into effect the realization that we stand, admittedly, always in the truth
of certain regions and stages; that, however, precisely even with this

manifestness of beings a concealedness of things is set and happens; yes, and what is more, a disguise and suppression, and that this untruth does not stand harmlessly as in a shed, next to truth, but that this untruth constantly rules our standing in the truth.

This truth about the truth is also true only for us. The addition "true for us" makes, however, no sense at all, since, to be sure, the regard to us belongs to truth.

With what has been briefly explained here, it is said how things stand with the truth of our questioning; that is, however, with the truth of philosophy. The opinion is frequently held that philosophy, as the highest science, must be devoid of a standpoint. One has wanted to raise this to a principle. However, there must be a standpoint; one cannot stand without standpoint. It is not about freedom from a standpoint, but about the fact that a standpoint is gained by fighting. It is about a decision of standpoint. This is not a matter of a philosophy that hovers in the clouds, but is a matter of the philosophizing human being, determined through his historical *Dasein*.

§ 17. The ambiguity of the word "history"

We have developed this question concerning the essence of truth, not accidentally, but necessarily, since it is very closely connected with the question concerning the essence of history. History is that which is distinctive for the being of the human being, [it] is the distinctive determination in the question concerning the essence of the human being.

If we now take up the question concerning the essence of history, one could think that we have arbitrarily decided what history is, namely, that history is that which is distinctive for the being of the human being. One could object, on the one hand, that there are human beings and human groups (Negros like, for example, Kaffirs) who have no history, of which we say that they are without history. On the other hand, however, animal and plant life has a thousand year long and eventful history. Fossils give an instructive evidence of this. Yes, not only life, under which we include the animal and the plant, but the entire earth also has its history. We do track this history, for example, the changes of the earth's crust. The geologist tracks the history of the earth in its ages. There is, therefore, history also outside the human region; on the other hand, within the human region, history can be missing, as with Negros. Therefore, history would be no distinctive determination of human being.

We cannot prohibit the use of the words "history of evolution" and "earth history." The question remains only, what do we mean there by "history." One speaks, after all, also of the history of Frederick the Great, the history of the peasants' war, the history of protestant theology. Do we understand here by "history" the same as in the forms of expression "history of the earth age" and "history of evolution of mammals"?

"History" and "history" is obviously not the same. If that is so, we must pursue this ambiguity and grasp it at the root; for here, it is not merely about an irregularity in the use of language. In this rather a certain wavering and an insecurity in the fundamental position toward the essential regions show themselves, which we pronounce and address in word usage, respectively. This insecurity points back to a peculiar uprooting of our being, in which we remain entangled and which we cannot fix through any standardization of the use of language.

a) "History" as entering into the past. Natural history
Do "history" and "history" mean the same? If yes: What then is history? If no: In which direction do the essential differences lie?

Here, as there, we can say that it is about occurrences, which in the manner of succeeding one another and acting upon one another operate in time and take up certain periods; that these thus characterized occurrences go by with time, that means, enter into the past and belong to history as that which has entered into the past. "History" means here, however, the temporal succession of the sequence of occurrences that sinks away into the past. This succession becomes a history in [its] going by. It is thereby indifferent in which region of occurrences this succession takes place.

If we take "history" thus, then nature too has history. If we put into effect this concept of history—"history" as sequence of occurrences that sinks away, then even the succession of the revolutions of the propeller on an aircraft is history. After all, something happens. And, yet, we resist talking about history here. We do set off precisely nature against history, [we] distinguish natural sciences and humanities. Cautiously, we do not name the latter "sciences of history"—and with this [we] are released from the difficulty that the geologist, who deals with earth history, and the zoologist, who deals with the history of evolution, belong to the scientists, and not to historians. Yet, where does mathematics, the allegedly most certain science, stand here? Is it a natural science, because it is used by physicists and chemists? Or is it a science of history, although the philologist can manage without it?

Even nature, the animate as well as the inanimate, has its history. But, how do we come to say that Kaffirs are without history? They have history just as well as the apes and the birds. Or do earth, plants, and animals possibly have after all no history? Admittedly, it seems indisputable that that which goes by, immediately belongs to the past; however, not everything that passes by and belongs to the past needs to enter into history.

What about the revolutions of the propeller? This might rotate day after day—yet, properly nothing happens thereby. If the aircraft, however, takes the *Führer* from Munich to Mussolini in Venice, then history happens. The flight is an historical happening, but not the running of the engine, although the flight can only happen while the engine runs. And, yet, not only the meeting of the two men is history, but the aircraft itself enters into history and is perhaps later someday set up in the museum. The historical character depends, however, not on the number of revolutions of the propeller, which have passed in time, but on the future happening resulting from this meeting of the two leaders.

b) "History" as entering into the future

To enter into history means, therefore, not simply that something that is bygone, merely because it is bygone, is classed with the past. Yes, it is, generally speaking, questionable whether the entering into history always means to be sent to the past, as it were. If a *Volk* without history enters into history, we mean by "history" not the past, but the future, which co-determines the *Volk* entering into history. Just as much, however, can this *Volk* also be placed out of history; it is, as it were, placed outside, placed on the strand, it has no more future. We have, therefore, that which is remarkable, the fact that a *Volk* enters into history (past) in that it is placed out of history (future).

History is ambiguous. And, how confusedly do we think about history and our own being, assuming that history constitutes the most proper character of our kind of being! It becomes clear that a *Volk* without history, which later enters into history, is without history in an entirely different sense than the earth. The earth can neither enter into history, nor step out of it; it has nothing to do with history. However, can it not all be the same? The southern Balkan Peninsula entered into history more than two thousand years ago. A mountain chain, a river can become [a] site for world-historical decisive battles. We speak of "historical soil," [we] say that an entire region is, as it were, laden with history.

The soil, therefore, also enters into history. However, the event of this entering into is no occurrence in the order of the succession of the changes in the earth's crust. Rather, the happening, in which the soil enters into, is history, is that which the Völker make. And the *Völker* do not enter into history, as if that were an available space in which they find lodging, a present-at-hand path, which they only would have to traverse, but "making history" means: *first to create the space and soil*. "Making" [*Machen*] does not mean here to produce, in the sense in which one can produce and preserve a thing. Although a *Volk* makes [*macht*] its history, this history is not, however, the work [*das Gemächte*] of the *Volk*; the *Volk* for its part is made [*gemacht*] by history.

With this, a new ambiguity arises here: A *Volk* carries its history before itself in its willing and yet, on the other hand, is carried by history. The first ambiguity—that the *Volk* enters into history, as it steps out of it—is connected with the second one. In any case, it becomes more distinct: History is not only succession of occurrences. That is why, strictly speaking, the earth also has no history. But why not?—Because the human being does not take part in that and because only the human being is historical. What in the human being is historical? The changing of the gastric juices, of the blood circulation, the graying of the hair—is that history? Or is that history, that a human being is procreated and born, ages and dies? That is also said to occur with dog and cat.

And yet, the hour of Albrecht Dürer's birth and the hour of Frederick the Great's death are history. If a dog perishes or a cat has a litter, that is no history; at best, an old aunt makes a history from that. Dürer's birth hour and Fredrick the Great's death hour are not, therefore, history because they have become subsequently (*post festum*) significant, but in itself the birth of the human being is already history.— What does that mean? The indication that it is about human things here cannot explain much to us first of all—especially since we are just about in the process of asking who the human being is. The appeal to the fact that history happens only where there are human beings renders us no service in this case.

We have confined history to the being of the human being. However, also nonhuman beings, like, for example, the mentioned aircraft of the *Führer*, can become historical through a peculiar entering into history, which presents a characteristic happening. We determine, with this restriction, *history as being of the human being,* and reject "animal history" and "earth history" as vacuous. History is a distinctive character of human being.

But, it is this human being [*dieses menschliche Sein*] that we shall understand precisely first from the concept of the essence of history! Thus, once again, we are going in a circle: We determine history from the human being and the human being from history. We are going in a circle and are, therefore, on the right way. It remains for us only the continuation of the way taken: the preliminary comparative consideration of human being as history in comparison with the non-historical being of the earth, of plants, and animals. It does not suffice to distinguish the movement of the earth crust and the life-processes, on one hand, and the human happening, on the other hand, in such a way that we only approximately and intuitively have an inkling of the distinction and surrender the rest to a phrase. The distinction must be comprehended as lying in the inner constitution of the realm of being concerned.

§ 18. Human happening as carrying itself out and
      remaining in knowing and willing: lore

The earth's changes are mechanically and physically determinable as drifts. Plant and animal life is a peculiar instinctual unity of a whole of life. The human happening, on the other hand, is *deliberate* and, therefore, *knowing,* and, in fact, not only each time *in itself,* so that knowing and will would be co-determinant for the human happening in its execution, but also insofar as this happening *remains* as happening in knowing and to a certain measure also in willing—that, consequently, a *lore* [Kunde] of that can remain preserved and that, therefore, this happening is *explorable* [erkundbar].

A hundred-year old forest not only has no records and reports, but it has in general no lore of its dying. The ants, which undertake raids, do not preserve them, they leave their past, as it were, behind themselves; they cannot even forget it, they have no lore of that which takes place with them. (This is to be established not empirically, but metaphysically.) On the other hand, in the deliberate and knowing happening of the human being, some lore [*Kunde*] always develops at the same time, in which it is attainable and always announces [*ankündigt*] itself again.

The Greeks have used the word ἱστορία for exploring [*das Erkunden*]. This word only received the meaning of "lore of history" ["*Geschichtskunde*"] in the course of their own history. The word means today as "Historiography," the knowing about history. *History* [Geschichte] is an event [*Ereignis*], insofar as it *happens* [geschieht]. A happening [*Geschehen*] is *historiographical*, insofar as it stands in some *lore* [Kunde], is *explored* [er*kundet*] and manifested [be*kundet*]. Is that which is historiographical only a supplement to the historical? Or is history only where there is historiography, so that the statement "No history without historiography" comes about?

Recapitulation
We asked about the essence of history. This question was recently, that is, in the past century, squeezed into the space of the philosophy of history—just like language in the space of the philosophy of language. We avoid this clamping of history for the same reasons for which we have avoided the clamping of language. Here, as there, an essential ground is *decisive*: History is no matter of a certain local region, but immediately intervenes in the ultimate questions of philosophical knowledge.

We have determined truth as the manifestness of beings, by virtue of which we are fitted and bound in that which is. We have disavowed an absolute truth. That does not mean, however, that we advocate the thesis of an only relative truth; relativity is merely arbitrariness. The rejection of the standpoint of the absolute truth means, at the same time, the rejection of all relations between absolute and relative. If one cannot speak in this sense of an absolute truth, neither can one speak of relative truth. The whole relation is askew.

We have formed, in the first place, the thesis "history is the distinctive kind of being of the human being." However, we have maintained reservations against this. Extra-human regions also have history; we thus talk about earth history and history of animal evolution. However, on the other hand, there are also races and *Völker* without history. The concept of history consequently proved itself ambiguous. What is generally meant here by "history"? Or what do we understand by "history," if we restrict the concept to the human being.

The broader concept of history means: succession elapsing in time, which sinks back into the past. With this, we can name every succession "history." We can pose the question from here, to what extent the revolutions of the propeller are history, and to what extent and in which sense can we ascribe history to an aircraft. The latter results only where human activity and happening are at play. We cannot, accordingly, speak of history with regard to animal and plant.

To establish clear concepts from the start: That which we in a very broad sense grasp as "history" means any kind of change. It is the most general concept of *movement*. We speak at one time of the mere *flow* of a mechanical happening; then—regarding a movement within the sphere of life—of *process*; we speak of *happening* [Geschehen] in the realm of the human (= history) [(=*Geschichte*)].

	Movement	
Flow	Process	Happening
(Earth)	(Life)	(Human being)

With this broader concept of history, we can say that also a *Volk* without history has history.

Though we cannot here systematically think through the individual forms of movement—flow, process, happening—the course of the questioning and of the contrast becomes, nevertheless, clear; it becomes in any case clear that only where the human being is—not as living being, but as human being—does history happen.

We must continue going on in this direction and carrying out the contrasting of this specifically human happening opposite the other realms of being more determinately. This being-moved, the moving of the human being, thus happens as one that is *deliberate* and thereby [as one] *that knows*. On the ground of the fact that this self-moving is one that is deliberate-knowing, it enters into a particular lore [*Kunde*] of itself and is, therefore, capable of being explored [*erkundbar*] and should be announced [*künden*] to others. We said that this lore belongs in general to history. If we substitute "lore" for the Greek word "historiography," then there is no history without historiography.

If we pursue this thesis with the intention of comprehending the happening as a peculiar kind of movement that is characterized by lore, a difficulty seems to open up: The happening, to be sure, is deliberate-knowing, but the will and the knowing alone do not determine histori-cal activities. This remains rather closely bound up with the power of the conditions, the contingencies—contingencies, taken as the gate through which the powers win admittance into the happening.

However, still then, if we observe this restriction, this emphasis on his-toriography, on the lore of history, remains obviously an impossibility:

1. History still must have happened each time, before it passes into a lore and continues to become object of a historiography.
2. History can happen, without our having lore of it. Much happens, of which we have no lore, and this happening is not the most unimportant.

Thus, the coupling of history and lore of history is as nonsensical perhaps as the statement: No nature without natural science. What does history care about the science of history? The latter is indeed dependent upon the former, but not conversely the former on the latter.

§19. The relationship of history, lore of history (historiography) and science of history

We have said, however: No history without *historiography*, from which follows that we do not equate historiography with the *science* of history, but grasp [it] deliberately in a broader sense. The science of history is the examining and organizing elaboration of an historical lore. It goes beyond a contingent experiencing of remarkable and acci-dental things, and aims for a complete connection of the happening and the presentation of the same. Lore (historiography in the Greek sense) is only the preform of the science of history. In the science of history, history must be an object. We will try to win insight into history by way of a discussion of the science of history.

From the above conception of the science of history, the noteworthy inference results: If the history of science brings the lore (historiography) into a complete connection and, if the lore belongs to our happening as such, then, however, an historical era must become more historical the more comprehensively and the more rigorously the ruling science of history expands and spreads itself. However, it is obviously not so. A blooming science with the greatest disposal over holdings of sources, with the most systematic organization, the most developed technology, and the most well prepared congresses can bring about the opposite and be a cutting off of history, a misjudgment of the historical happening and a paralysis and reversal of the historical being.

We are talking here, however, not about mere possibility, but about facts. "Historians" (history scientists) have had the most difficulty and were the latest to comprehend how history happens, not, as one might suppose, because they "are of a different mind with regard to politics," but because they are precisely historians, historians, as the present science of history has trained them for decades. This shall be no disparaging of the science. However, we must be aware of this: Not everyone who works in an archive, not every professor, not every secondary school teacher lecturing on history is already a historian in the original sense of the word, that is, with an essential relation to history. To be sure, we use this expression also in the broader sense, and "historian" then means those who occupy themselves with the *science* of history. (And sometimes we understand by "history" even a Saint Nicholas celebration that turned out well.)

However, history scientists can lock themselves and us out of history—as there are also those who occupy themselves with medicine and are no physicians, those who occupy themselves with philosophy all their life and never become philosophers. "Historian" can be the person who looks after merely the reputation, flourishing, and success of the *science*; the fact that the object of this science is then also *there* is thereby actually irrelevant.

However, have we not refuted our statement "No history without historiography" with such a reference to the worthiness of question of the science of history? The historiography that is organized by the science of history can in fact stand apart from history, impair its understanding, and accordingly not stand in history, hampering and thwarting it. However, is this thwarting and hampering of the historical being perhaps no relationship to history? Is this disastrous and perseverant happening not just rather a proof of our statement that history is co-determined by lore?

On the other hand, it follows that the science of history, as it can have a hampering relationship, also can have one that is supportive. It only depends on *creating* such a relationship. The presupposition for that is that clarity prevails over how [the] science of history relates to lore, whether science presents the higher form of lore or vice versa, whether the science of history becomes determined only with respect to the genuineness and clarity of the lore, indeed that *this* [lore] first decides whether [the] science of history is necessary or not.

In itself, [the] science of history is just as little necessary as any other science, especially since something can be incorrect historically-scientifically, which as *lore* of history is, nevertheless, very impor-tant—a possibility before which the philistine must shudder. (Fortunately, he is not the object of history.)

(For example, it was a blunder of the science of history, as it tried to refute Spengler's work "The Decline of the West." In this, it was, to be sure, largely successful. Nothing, however, has changed with this; the mood of decline was, nevertheless, further facilitated, and in a brief time span, the science worked in Spengler's lines of sight. The worth of Spengler's work is not confirmed by the large number of copies; this speaks rather for the inane feeblemindedness of the public.)

The correctness of historical-scientific knowledge does not yet guarantee the truth of a lore; conversely, just as little must that which is historical-scientifically incorrect be operative historically and as lore.

From all this, it becomes doubtful whether we experience from the science of history that which is essential about history. For that reason, the relationship of the science of history to the lore of history must be determined more closely.

By *lore of history*, we understand the *respective manner of the mani-festness, in which an era stands in history*, in such a way, to be sure, that this manifestness also carries and leads the historical being of the era.

How does the thus understood lore relate to the science of histo-ry?—We do not want to give here a formal definition of the science of history. The characterization of today's predominant scientific stance suffices. The latter determines itself out of the leading conception of science in general. The concept of science arises from the leading con-ception of knowledge. The concept of knowledge is grounded in the respective understanding and the respective understanding of the essence of truth. The essence of truth results from the fundamental position of the human being in the whole of being. This fundamental position is ruled by the manner in which the human being stands in that which is; it is ruled by *who* the human being is and whether and how the human being asks and replies to this question. That is, therefore, the decision, in which *we ourselves* stand.

This whole connection cannot be discussed thoroughly in detail, but must stay in sight, if we raise the question concerning science. Today's conception of science depends upon the dominant concept of truth: the correspondence of the proposition with the object. Science must, therefore, be objective, and all means and ways of experience are made serviceable for this striving after objectivity. It is important that the succession, the intertwinings and the interlinkings of history are presented in the most unbroken way possible to observe all circumstances and effects and to present all this in complete impartiality.

The human being—his works and achievements, his deeds and failures—stands at the center of the happening of history; thus, the necessity arises of being informed in a sufficiently objective manner about the human being. For that reason, it is recommended to occupy oneself with psychology and characterology, possibly also with psychoanalysis. Since the human being, however, also lives in society, one has in addition built sociology over that. Many historians, on the other hand, dispense with psychology and society and search for human knowledge, which they apparently need, in the great poets, in the great figures of history, in biographies. Others again, content themselves with the everyday-natural knowledge of the human being and rely on common sense. The historian must, then, take a bearing on his objects, as it were, according to the respective human image and the leading image of human things, and the presentation and the kind of research—down to the critique of sources—would turn out depending on this respective image.

Even if a historian arranges the whole intertwining of the causes and works on all of the connections, as, for example, the 1807 collapse of Prussia—it can, despite the objectivity, remain questionable whether a lore of the happening at that time is gained and conveyed in his work. Though the reviewer can report in detail that the work presents a great advance, and the teacher at the Gymnasium reaches for it in order to make use of it in class—his boys can be bored nevertheless and be led scientifically past this era . They will not receive a lore of this [history] because the teacher has no lore, but holds in his hands a work of scientific ambition.

Why is this lore, of which one believes it may be something familiar, missing? Because one cares about the increase in the literature *about* things, and not about the history, that is, *the things themselves.* Why does history remain a dead object? Because the historians are not capable of making history alive and true, because they do not bring it into relation with the present. They do not try. They stay in the science and tend to its blossoming. They depict away a mere then.

Why, however, shall something bygone become livelier in relation to the present? In this case, there would, of course, be the presupposition that the present is lively experienced in an historical manner. Or does one believe that that which is of the present and that which is of today stand, as it were, by themselves before the eyes and nose, while that which is bygone is gone? That is, of course, in a certain manner, correct. A swirl of events, an uncounted fullness of facts is immediately graspable in that which is of today. However, who guarantees that this happening, of which we say that something is "going on," is *history* and not the merely everyday great variety of things?

If a historian takes up this that is of today, and presents [it] with journalistic skill, and for that purpose relates the past [to it] and ascertains correspondences, for example, characterizes Xenophon as "Major"—will he make the past history more lifelike through this? Perhaps the history of the present is even more difficult to grasp than that of the past, for we have, to be sure, a certain distance with regard to the past, and one needs the distance in order to see an object—though not distance alone; otherwise, it would have to be that the farther back something lies, the more objectively it could be presented.

On the other hand, that which is invidious does not yet lie in the fact that the historian looks at that which is present, respectively, and places it in relation to the past. It lies rather *wherein* the present history is experienced. In every happening, there is that which makes noise and racket, there is window-dressing, idle talk, bustle, machination, enterprise, semblance of accidents, passion of the unrestrained, the formless, the daily ascertainable events. All of that belongs to history as necessarily as the valley to the mountain. And yet, that is not in the proper sense history, but unhistory. This that is unhistorical is to be sharply separated from that which is without history. The life of plant and animal can never be unhistorical, because it does not know a *happening* as kind of being. There is unhistory only where happening is. However, this happening does not always need to be history.

What we name unhistory here should not be, in spite of the negative expression, perhaps disparaged or morally devalued. That which is historical cannot be comprehended with the standards *good* and *evil*. Something morally good can be very unhistorical, and something immoral can be very historical. Good and evil are just as little standards for the happening as progress and regress.

This that is unhistorical steps now at first into the horizon. The reference to that which is unhistorical can, to be sure, make the presentation more comprehensible, but in no way does history need to be grasped with this. Within the past, often only that which is unhistorical becomes graspable at first, the so-called *facts* and what one has talked about them and meant. This that is unhistorical is that which can be made into an object at the very first and most easily. For this reason, the "objectivity" of the science of history still does not need to guarantee any lore of the happening.

The lore of history is, therefore, so closely bound up with history in a mysterious way that we are not, in fact, able to penetrate this relationship by way of the science. Assuming that lore belongs to the inner constitution of the historical happening, then we must make clear *from the happening*, to what extent something like lore can belong to this kind of being [*Seins*]. The question concerning the relationship of lore to history can be circumscribed so far on the basis of what has been gained up to now so that we comprehend the inner belongingness of lore to history as such.

Recapitulation

With our question concerning the essence of history we have come to a decisive point in the entire question connection, so that it appears fitting to visualize this connection, even if only wholly in an external way, through a listing of the essential key words. We have set for ourselves the task of thematizing *logic*. This has the *Logos* as theme, which we determined as *language*. The question arose: "What and how is language, and to which realm of being does it belong?" Language is a distinctive determination of the *human being*. That is why we asked: "What is the human being?" The question "What is the human being?"

has changed into the question "Who are we *Ourselves*?" "Ourselves," spelled in capital letters, for the self-character is that which is essential.

The first answer that we gave read "*Volk*." We have characterized this answer at the same time as answer that is *after the manner of decision*. We have understood the essence of decision in *resoluteness*. Resoluteness however, is not a single act, but a *happening*, by virtue of which we are fitted in the happening in which we stand. From this, the question arose: "What is *history*?"

Logic

Logos

Language

Human being

Who are we ourselves?

Volk

Decision

Resoluteness

What is history?

If we take the *course* of the questions as that which is decisive, then we have, so to speak, encountered ourselves out of the greatest possible conceptual breadth (namely, of thinking) to the ever more constricting concepts and with the point of the question; and from this question concerning ourselves we came again into the expanse up to the question concerning history, in which we stand. We have not strayed from the beginning thereby, but we can at any time turn around the sequence of the questioning so that we arrive again at the beginning. The sequence of the question must be renewed continuously, especially with regard to *philosophical* questioning. Every answer here also places into question again that which has been attained until now. It is different in *science*.

We have applied the question concerning history and its essence in such a manner that we have first of all taken history in a very broad sense: history of the earth, of the living beings. We have seen at the same time that this broad concept of history as *flow* of the past is admittedly justified, that the concept in this broad sense is, nevertheless, not sufficient for the special characterization of history in the narrower sense of the one in which the human being takes part. History was contrasted with movement in the sense of *flow* and of *process*, insofar as with history it is about the human being, and the happening that is born by human being is always also one that is deliberate and knowing.

From this determination, a peculiar connection between history and manifestness of history, that is, *lore of history*, had to be contemplated. We have made it a habit to affirm an essential connection between history and lore of history.

The closer consideration led to going into the question concerning the *science of history*. This is a certain formation of lore, ordered in certain regards, critically examining, encompassing; it can be exemplary in the execution. In spite of all that, the science of history does not guarantee immediately the access to history, but it can be that the science of history shields us precisely from history; however, a leading and a transferring into the historical happening is also possible just as well—if it corresponds to that with which it deals. We saw, at the same time, that today's science of history and that of the nineteenth century stand under the essential influence *of* the concept of truth, according to which, truth is the correspondence of proposition and object. The fact that objectivity and factuality are a necessary determination of the science of history is not disputed by us. The question is only, how, and as what, is the object determined.

It was not doubtful that the human being stands at the center of history. Hence, in the nineteenth century, the claim was made that historical research should be based on psychology, characterology, sociology. That was also the reason for the foundation of the Lamprecht-Institute in Leipzig. In spite of that, this grotesque idea could not last, although with a wider public, this position was still recently championed.

The question was, accordingly, how the science of history can be grounded originally, so that it is perfect, as it were, according to its own laws. Yet, even if that is attained, as is affirmed today, it can, nonetheless, be that the science of history does not properly come close to history, that, for it, history remains a dead object.

We saw, however, that the demand to bring the science of history into relation with the present is doubtful. That is to say, if we pursue that which is of today in its happening—with the intention of grasping the proper history by that—then it appears that all historical happening carries with it an unhistory: that which is inevitable, that which is everyday. This unhistory is nothing negative; it relates to history like the valley to the mountain. This unhistory is not, however, restricted to the present, but merges equally into the past, and here it is, yet again, that which catches the eye in this [past] first of all.

The result of these interpretations shows, accordingly, that the happening as such is unhistorical and, at the same time, also properly historical; history carries this ambiguity in itself in a concealed manner.

§20. History in its relationship with time

We now will orient our questioning concerning the essence of history only to the happening in order to grasp history's character of happening. The question concerning lore is thereby to be put aside.

In our deliberations, we have made use throughout of a characterization of history, which is the most common, so that we do not at all scrutinize it further, namely, the characterization of history as that which is *bygone*. It is, therefore, a matter of history in its relationship with time. To be sure, the discussion of the relation of the science of history to time has led to the fact that not only the past, but also the present, play a role for the historical being [*Sein*], namely, not only for livening up the presentation; it was claimed, rather, that the respective historical present reached each time is, as it were, the reference point for the happening that has lapsed. Present and past, therefore, characterize history. On the other hand, the third realm, the future, is apparently left out in the question concerning the essence of history.

We can explain this to ourselves with the relationship of the *science* of history with *time*. One can charge the historian to include the present, but one cannot expect of him to include the future—he would actually have to be a prophet or soothsayer. Experientially, things indeed happen differently than one thinks. So, this soothsaying is not only impossible, but it would also be confusing and entirely useless.

The science of history is, however, already a determinate *expansion* of the lore of history. History and the determination of the historical itself cannot, however, be carried out entirely without the third realm, the future. For, if we perhaps say that hitherto unhistorical *Völker* enter into history and from now on become co-determinant for the future, then it is obvious that history and happening are determined with respect to past, present, and future.

The discussion of the relationship of history and time can lead to an essential determination of history. Yet, the reference of history to time is so obvious and self-evident that we almost have misgivings in expressing our opinions about it. For, not only the happening in history, but also the happening in the broadest sense, any kind of movement does elapse in time. With this, *any* kind of movement can be determined with respect to time, indeed [it can] also be *calculated*. What follows from this?—The fact that with reference to time we do not get to grasp that which is *distinctive* of history. After all, the movement of the living and the lifeless in nature (process and flow) also elapses in time.

The *tempus* factor occurs as the one that co-determines each happening, each kind of movement. One has grasped time even as fourth coordinate, as fourth dimension, and has spoken of a four-dimensional world. In it, [it] is revealed that any kind of movement is determinable by time, whereby the numerical kind of determination of the time-character can be different, according to the realm. The science of history that calculates with time cannot, to be sure, specify the *t* factor by which a time-duration is defined, but doubtless, [it can specify] history numbers as the calendar-like declarations of data. However, although tempus and historical number are different in their character of determination, time is nevertheless always represented as a framework and a dimension in the case of nature and history, within which movement takes place in a sequence and is, accordingly, determinable in terms of position.

Observed from here, we do not yet see the characteristic distinction between nature-happening and history. One could say that in the investigation of nature, the time-determination plays a much more essential role than in the science of history; and, yet, with this, the relationship of history and time is still not grasped in what is essential, and [is] not fully grasped.

If time already constitutes an element of determination of nature and history—how is it then that one simply determines history, of all things, through time? We do say: history is that which is bygone. We never speak in this sense with regard to nature, we never say it is that which is bygone or that which is futural; at most we say, it is that which is present. If, however, we say, "the city has a great past," we thus mean a great history.

Likewise, the demand that history must be placed in relation to the present points to the fact that here too we mean history as past. History is determined here downright as time-realm. It is evident that here time is not only an indifferent framework for the flow of the happening.

What about the relationship of history and time? We pose three questions with the expectation of hitting upon the character of happening of history with this:

1. What does it mean, if we say that history is that which is bygone? How is the time-determination *past* properly meant here?
2. How is it that in the characterization of happening with reference to time the past, of all things, assumes this peculiar preeminence?
3. What results from the reply to both previous questions for the determination of the relationship of history and time?

a) History as that which is bygone and as that which has been

To 1.: How is *past* to be understood here? We can generally say: Only the happening that has happened, that is *perfect*, stands in the past (in the *perfectum*), is that which is bygone and, as such, [is a] possible object of the science of history. Yet, here the question follows whether the science of history does, in fact, make the past alone into an object, whether it only aims at the bygone, the decaying and the coming to nothing. That is *not* correct. For, even where the decline of a State or of an era is investigated, yes, even where history is fundamentally thought of as history of decline, it does not depend only on the emphasis on the coming into being and becoming of the decline. The historical reflection pursues that which once was, but not only in its going by, but also in its becoming and having-become. In this having-become, lies something that continues to operate decisively and points beyond it.

That which is bygone is not simply that which goes by, but that which still remains, that which continues to be effective, from earlier on still being somehow, which from earlier on still essences, goes on in its own way, that which *still essences* or *that which has been*. That which has been is, to be sure, always something that is bygone, but not everything that is bygone is that which has been in the sense of that which essences from earlier on; therefore, on the one hand, that which is *bygone* and, on the other hand, *that which has been* and *still essences*. In this way, the time-determination is subject to the characterization of that which goes by, but also [to the characterization] of essence.

Both titles, "past" and "beenness," are not merely two different words that we use arbitrarily. We can use both words in a similar sense and thus without thinking, but here it depends neither on our opinion nor on the *word*, but on the *matter*. In thinking of the past, we see in the direction of the gliding-away of time out of the present into the realm of the going by, of the coming to nothing. With beenness, we look conversely from what has become into the present. In the first case, we take time as something stepping away from the future over the present into the past. In the other case, we take time as something advancing from the past over the present beyond into the future. We have here a strange doubling of the idea of the passing of time. We thus see that the historical-scientific thinking works with a peculiar coupling of both time-concepts.

If history is characterized predominantly as past, then that does not exclude that the passing of time in the opposite direction is missed. One can thereby represent time in the image of a line. It seems arbitrary in which direction we look at the timeline, in which direction we run along in time and let the events flow. All the more pressing is the second question.

b) The preeminence of the characterization of history as past

To 2.: Why does precisely the past have this remarkable and, for us, so self-evident preeminence in the characterization of history, and whence comes this preeminence? This question is divided into two parts:

a) Why has the past preeminence for us for a long time in the characterization of that which once was, over that which we name *beenness*?

b) Why does what is thus understood as that which once was serve, of all things, for the characterization of history?

α) Christian world-conception and Aristotelian time-analysis

To a): Two reasons are responsible for this: 1. the influence and the dominance of the Christian world-conception, 2. the kind and direction of the first decisive philosophical thinking about time (Aristotle).

We cannot discuss extensively here, as with so much, these two main reasons. We note however:

1. For the Christian world-conception, the proper being is God as that which is uncreated, eternal. That which we call "the world" is created from out of him. With the world and, simultaneously with it, time is created; it is in the manner of a creature. All that

which has been created is that which is transient. So, transience is equated with temporality: that which is temporal is that which is transient, that which goes by. That is why everything is determined by time, that we experience the human being itself, situated in time, in advance as transient.

2. The influence of the first decisive philosophical determination of the essence of time: the treatise by Aristotle, *Physics*, Book IV, Chap. 10.

It is a natural way of proceeding that, in the first reflection on what time is, the latter is grasped where we have it, in a manner of speaking, unshortened, namely, in the now. The now is that which is in time, which is present and is in the manner of being present; that which is futural is the not yet; the bygone, that which is no more. However, since then, for us, the now is the substance of time, which, to be sure, has the peculiarity of disappearing already immediately in each now. The immediate experience in this connection is that this now even now is no longer now, that it goes by.

On the ground of this idea of the time-flow from the now, time inspires the fundamental impression of passing and, therefore, Aristotle also says (Book IV, chap. 13, 222 b19 sq.): "Time is, therefore, in itself more to blame that something goes by than that something comes into being."

The φθορά is in the power of time. Hegel says, accordingly: Time is that which consumes. He sees time in the flow into the past. That is expressed also in the natural manner of speech "Time goes by." (However, it does not say "Time comes into being.") Time is that which goes by in the distinctive sense. This is why all that stands in it, the human things and the human being himself, is that which is transient. We gather from this that we think, as it were, in the coupling of the Christian and of the ancient world-conception. Today, we move just as if it were a matter of course in the representation of time that has emerged from this coupling.

β) That which is bygone as that which is completed, ascertainable, causally explicable

To b): Why does that which once was understood as past, serve precisely for the characterization of history? History does take interest precisely in becoming, that is, in the coming into being, in the connections of development. How is it that, in spite of the fact that history is oriented ahead, the past also dominates in history?—The reason is that that which is bygone is, as it were, that which is completed, the finished; that, with the Greeks, that which is earlier and once was, that which has come to conclusion, as γενόμενον, which as such in a certain way still has a mode of staying, becomes proverbial for the time-concept. That which is completed is that which dates back. As such, it offers for the customary conception of the determining and experiencing of objects the realm for a science. That which is bygone as that which is completed lies in the realm of *ascertainability*, insofar as in history it is a matter not only of explaining an extant bygone, but also of going back further over an extant bygone toward one that lies still farther back, [toward a] still earlier one.

The going back into that which is more and more bygone becomes intensified by the tendency to search for the cause. If the cause-connection is emphasized sufficiently, then history is understood. However, the opposite is the case. The greatest error is to believe that history is and is ever to be comprehended on the basis of causal connections.

c) The objectification of history by the science of history.
Time as present-at-hand framework
To 3.: What results now from the response to both of the first questions for the third, hence, for the knowledge of the relationship of history and time?—In order to answer this question, we must combine what we have said separately about the preeminence of the past. There are two tendencies that at bottom run opposite one another, which have solidified the idea of history as past: 1. the conception that understands happening as going by, 2. the aim of the science of history to make into a topic and object this that is bygone as that which is put down and still today is that which is extant.

That which is bygone is that which is fixed, that which is finished, that which is utterly inalterable—in this conception, the past has, in what concerns the inalterability of its laws, a character corresponding to nature. Through this conception, that which is bygone becomes *objectifiable*; thereby history first becomes an *object,* insofar as the fixation of that which is extant in the manner of standing opposite is understood by that.

The science of history has an interest in pressing back and fastening the happening as far as possible into the past. Only thus can it present it. Thus, what is dependent upon the science of history and its line of question is not only the selection and the historical content, not only the kind and the direction, as well as the respects for the explanation and investigation of what is historical, but [also] the science of history as history essentially participates in the fact that history is ascertained as that which is bygone.

The view on that which is *transient* and the view on that which is *objective*, therefore, unite here. We gather from this that history in this conception is represented as a present-at-hand flow that is in itself stable, as it were. And time is here a present-at-hand framework, a present-at-hand course on which the happening flows. It is a problem that both, happening and time, disappear into the past. From this, the task arises to preserve them in some form, to save it in tradition. Time itself is represented as present and this [present] is thought as the extended and expanded now, that which is present-at-hand, that which is of today, that which is immediately graspable, [that] about which one can talk, so that the strange demand that the past must be placed in relation to the present, fundamentally makes no distinction between past and present; both become joined as that which in a certain way is on hand to us.

What have we attained now for the question to what extent is history that which is distinctive to the human being and to what extent does lore belong to history? Our result is nil. It has been confirmed that in the field of the history of the human being the same succession in the movement of coming into being and going by dominates, as in the regions of non-human being, of the being of the living being and of the earth. No wonder that, given this conception, we can safely talk of earth history and animal history too. It is not, however, the case that geology and zoology provide a particular concept of history, which we transfer to the history of the human being. On the contrary: the prevailing concept of history is so indeterminate that here too we can talk of history. History is understood here as *present-at-hand object*, which, precisely like time, somehow flows. The knowledge of history, as well as the knowledge of nature, are as it were, screwed on history and nature, like an apparatus through which the object, the happening, is ascertained.

Thus, the question concerning the relationship of history and time is not of much help. We fall into [the] danger of stating mere truisms here.

However, we cannot emphasize enough that history—as well as time—is conceived here as course, as course, which we set away from ourselves, yes, and, what is more, that one's own present is conceived as something that is set away, somehow present-at-hand, which takes place before us and of which one takes notice. This conception is almost second nature to us. We see no possibility of thinking and asking differently.

§ 21. The being of the human being as historical

Nonetheless, we must ask differently—without thereby denying even for an instant that which is peculiarly self-evident and passing it over in thinking. We must ask: How does it come about that this self-evident conception has such preeminence? And which possibility and necessity is there of breaking this self-evidence? How does it come about that we have still not reached what we search for, namely, to comprehend history as distinctive being of the human being?

The answers that we gave were inadequate because our understanding for [*Verständnis für*] history as being of the human being—and this being [*Sein*] understood as happening—was inadequate. We have, to be sure, made clear that the question concerning the human being must be posed as Who-question—"Who are we ourselves?"—and we have submitted an answer—"We are the *Volk*"—however, this answer has become questionable to us too, as we ascertained that "*Volk*" is understood as body, soul, spirit. The traditional representation of the human being as a living creature endowed with reason that occurs among other living beings repeated itself here after all.

Now we affirm that the being of the human being is historical. We should have learned that this proposition is captious as well. As we already heard, the proposition "We are we ourselves" can be correct and, yet, untrue—insofar as we are not we ourselves, but are caught up in self-forlornness. So, the proposition "We are historical" could now also be correct and untrue.

a) "Are" we historical?
The proposition "We are historical" is to be posed for this reason as question: "Are we historical?" It seems to be exaggerated caution, almost pathological distrust, if we call that into question. We are truly

enough tossed and turned in history through collapse, inner confusion, beset by external enemies and inner powers, at the mercy of the world-happening. The question "Are we historical?" here sounds almost like a mockery, if one understands historical being in the sense in which we have understood it up to now: to be an element within the happening of the incidents, which we can ascertain, and of which we get reports continuously. For what does one have the radio? One turns it on, and in ten minutes, one can learn "what is going on"; then, one turns it off again. Being-historical means then to be thrown around within the bustle.

"Are we historical?" Who would dream of saying "no" here? Everyone is informed about that and can easily make infallible comments. The question "Are we historical?" is superfluous, if we only understand it in that way as it easily enters our ears. We close our minds with this, however, to another meaning, which the question "Are we historical?" takes as a basis, namely, the one whether our being, which we ourselves are, comes to pass historically or whether we are only the observers, assessors, spectators and the know-it-all. We close our minds, therefore, to the meaning that the being of our Self is a happening and, with that, history.

We can understand the question in that manner. But, how shall we decide whether our being is historical?

b) The worthiness of question of the being of the human being.
  Becoming and being
Our being, the being of our selves—have we reflected on that before? Or is it enough that we just *are*? Admittedly, we have not always been and will also not always be the individuals in any case, but for a certain time-span here on the earth we have, nevertheless, a place, somewhere to stay. Our staying is our being. We *are*, that is, in time—from one point in time on, which one can later communicate to us, up to another, which none of us knows, but, which all the same, is fixed for each one of us. Our being is history; our limited, though constant presence on the earth is something that can be ascertained anytime by anyone. The police can ascertain, Mr. X is there, he exists.

Our being is a matter of course. We have certainly come into being and will go by, but as long as we say "we," we are. We are a staying subsistence as beings, transposed among other beings, of similar or different kind, human beings or animals and plants. With all these beings, with what remains and subsists there, just as with us, certain changes occur in the course of time. While we are, something changes, but our *being* stays, it is not subject to the change. The fact that we are as beings remains precisely the presupposition [*Voraussetzung*] for the fact that we are exposed [*ausgesetzt*] to all sorts of change.

This is how it stands with the happening too. What we call "happening," no matter whether in a narrower or in a wider sense, is movement, a becoming-other, a becoming. If we thus ask "Are we historical?" and, if we understand this question in the sense of whether our being is a happening, then it turns out from the start that this is an impossible question. For, happening is becoming, and "becoming" is the counter-concept of "being." The concept of being excludes becoming and happening.

And the fact that "becoming" is the counter-concept of "being," is an ancient insight, as ancient as philosophy, as ancient as the reflection on beings and being. Philosophy started with the Greeks precisely with this, that this original opposition of being and becoming was recognized and established. For, what first *becomes*, what must first go through a becoming, *is* not yet; what *is* needs no longer to *become*. Being and becoming are inseparable and incompatible—like fire and water. From the original beginning, all is determined by being and becoming. Both great thinkers, Heraclitus and Parmenides, move with their fundamental conceptions and principles precisely in this original opposition, which henceforth dominates all questioning of western philosophy up to the present. Nietzsche is in his actual fundamental position determined by this opposition, and in fact entirely deliberately.

Parmenides says: beings are, and nonbeings are not. All becoming, hence coming into being and going by, is a not-yet and no-more. All becoming is burdened with a not, is not-like, null. Against this, Heraclitus says, πάντα ῥεῖ, "All a becoming, a constant becoming." There is no being. So too Nietzsche: There is only a becoming, and being and the Is [*das Ist*] remain a semblance. The ground of this semblance is *logic*, which even where it speaks about becoming, solidifies and hardens all things in word meanings. The world that is, is illusion; there is only a world that becomes. What dominates western thinking in this manner is in our everyday understanding present and alive any time. Such oppositions as being and semblance, being and becoming are familiar to us. Being always means: Being completed, staying, constant remaining, subsisting, completion.

The fact that we are historical in the first sense, that fact that we take place, therefore, as present-at-hand within incidents, is not in dispute. The fact that we are historical in the second sense, the fact, therefore, that our being itself may be a happening, is nonsensical, understood from the original opposition of being and becoming. And, yet, the question remains, whether the above concept of being, constant remaining, with all its venerability and intimacy, is actually true. It remains as further question, whether the manner of the historical being, in which we commonly understand history—historical being as being of incidents—does not present the self-forlornness within the historical, that which we earlier named unhistory, a certainly necessary kind of historical being, but not the only one and the proper one.

Furthermore, the question arises whether a proper historical being is possible and, if yes, how it is possible, and what then does being mean in general, and how this understanding of being relates to *the* understanding of being in which we daily move.

The question sounds easy. And yet the difficulty arises of how to find out whether and how there are still other manners of historical being, whether and how the truth about being must be grasped differently.

Notwithstanding the fact that no way toward the answer is seen, we must realize that this original opposition of being and becoming that is so familiar to us today, was also once established and pronounced, not as an arbitrary fancy, but on the ground of a first and free resoluteness of the human being to take up an essential fundamental position for himself in the midst of beings and thus to comprehend being. Accordingly, our question and our task of grasping the truth about being will neither be able to be based in assessments of and discussions about a concept; question and answer will enclose a total transformation of our being in itself, which is itself a necessity of history, assuming that we are historical. If a new concept of history should disclose itself to us in this context, then the familiar representation of history is not uprooted with this, but only made manifest in its necessity and its captiousness.

c) Being-historical as a deciding that is continually renewing
It will become clear that being-historical is nothing that one carries around with oneself like a hat; it is rather a deciding that is continually renewing between history and unhistory in which we stand. With the

execution of the decision, we are raised to a higher rank of decision, so that our being experiences a higher form, greater sharpness, a different breadth and a final singularity.

Through this, that erroneous main result of all science of history, which paralyzes our relation to history and which pronounces itself in the statement "There is nothing new under the sun," is brought to nothing, This main result of all knowledge of history issues a confirmation to us, on the ground of which we can conveniently squeeze by all that which is unusual. "There is, after all, nothing new under the sun"—the statement becomes a certificate of the unpower of a time; it provides to knowledge the semblance of superiority and solidifies a condition, which I would like to call the condition of historical indolence. This indolence arises precisely out of the greatest possible historical knowledge.

It is not the condition of an individual, it lies over entire eras, precisely when one surveys and has a command of the whole world, the history of all lands and epochs. We have had until now no era in which all historical happening was as apparent as in ours. On the other hand, however, no era is as unhistorical as ours either, and in none has the historical indolence become as great as in ours.

Recapitulation

In order to secure the connection, we want to establish anew the whole context. In the beginning, we determined logic as the question concerning the essence of language. We made this determination in the distinction from the traditional logic as doctrine of the form and laws of thinking. With this, we have not only established the object of logic differently than hitherto, but we have also entered into another method of treating the topic.

The method of treating the topic of language is no doctrine, but a questioning, that is, an essential questioning. The question of the essence, however, is always a fore-question. The fore-question reads, "In which realm does language belong, and what is language?" In the pursuit of this question, we gained the insight: Language lies in the realm of the being of the human being.

So, we asked further, "What is the human being?" And, then, "Who is the human being?" The human being is historical. "What is history?" History is the distinctive being of the human being and, with this, of language.

The discussion of our question of what is language stands now in the realm of the question of what is history. We searched for the determination of the essence of history in the connection of history with time. By referring to time, however, we have not attained any distinctive mark for historical being, so long as we comprehend the time of natural processes and the time of history in a similar way.

Our questioning concerning history up to now yielded that history can no longer be an object, a being, about which we ask, but that it is a manner of being. We understand historical being as [a] basic mode of being. History is not a title for a being, but a mode of being [*Seinsart*].

However, in this context, the objection arose, whether history may be conceived as *happening* in the sense of a being [*eines Seins*]—insofar as happening, to be sure, is a becoming, and being precisely the counter-concept to becoming. Being and becoming exclude each other; there-fore, being and happening must also exclude each other. Accordingly, it seemed that history could not possibly be comprehended as being.

Now, one had to ask about the essence of the being of history. This question thus compels us to win the concept of history in such a way that we do not investigate the historical processes in their peculiarity with regard to the contents, but that we seek to comprehend historical being. We begin with the customary characterization of history as that which is bygone, as past. Such thinking takes past, however, not first as transience, but it is concerned about preserving and retaining the earlier actuality. Yet, there is already another sense of that which is bygone, if it is not meant in its going by, but in its former having-become, if it is understood as becomeness.

We arrive from there at a further possibility, namely, at the concept of history as that which *has been*, that is, that which still essences from earlier on.

That which is earlier was, therefore, conceived in a threefold manner:

1. as gone by,
2. as become,
3. as been.

If we follow the distinction between past, becomeness and beenness, then we arrive at another foundation, namely, of history no longer as an object, but as a happening, as our, the *Volk*'s, being. That which has been is not an empty time-determination; beenness is not an indifferent space for storage, but it is that which essences from earlier on, that is, that which essences of our own essence.

d) That which has been is as future of our own being

That which essences from earlier on, what is that? Perhaps that which today is still effective from the past? There is also naturally such a thing, insofar as we constantly stand under many aftereffects, which, as such, are also enumerable. The assessment of that which is still effective, how- ever, will depend on that which we experience in general as effective. We find, for example, decline, impotence, mediocrity, distress, depres- sion still effective; all this is effective, but, nonetheless, not essential for us. Therefore, that which is essential is not to be determined from that which is effective. Every era has its unessence, its unhistory. That must be so. No light is without shadow. However, who sees only the shadows and is horrified by that has not comprehended the light. To the towering height belongs the crash. History is no obstacle-free stroll into the future.

That which is effective in the present is not, therefore, the realm that can assure us what since earlier still essences. The unessence has the peculiarity that it does not let the essence arise; that it, however, itself tries to erect by itself the semblance of an essence. The unessence would be a matter of indifference, not worth the effort and easily visi- ble at a glance, if unessence were similar in meaning with non-essence. However, unessence is always the semblance of the essence, and it appeals to our craving for recognition, bewitches what we do and do not do, even with seemingly good intention. So also is true leadership [*Führung*] falsified, which then spreads as leading astray [*Verführung*].

With this, it should become clear that we cannot take up our essence in the sense in which we reach for the door handle. We can gain our essence only from that which is essential to us in the historical moment. That which is essential to us determines itself in a kind of knowing of its own, and it is not knowable as physical data are knowable. We expe- rience that which is essential only from the How and For What of our self-decision, *who* we want to become in the future, what we want to place under our command as that which is our future. *That which essences from earlier on determines itself from our future.*

However, the determination of this future is not subject to a predic- tion; it cannot be invented and concocted in a freely suspended manner.

It determines itself, rather, from that which essences from earlier on. That which essences from earlier on determines itself from the future; the future determines itself from what essences since earlier.

However, beenness may not be comprehended [*begriffen*] as past. That which essences from earlier on has its peculiarity to it in that it has always already grasped over [*hinweggegriffen*] every today and now: It *essences as tradition.*

This tradition [*Überlieferung*] is no inventory of experiences or reports, but it is the innermost character of our historicity. Through it, our own determination is carried off over [*über*] ourselves, through it we are delivered [*ausgeliefert*] into the future. That which essences comes up toward us [*kommt auf uns zu*] in this reaching over [*Übergriff*] from the future [*Zukunft*]. For this reason, we name this happening *die "Zukunft"* [the "future"]. It comes to us not of itself, but only when we are capable of following the tradition, of taking it over [*sie zu übernehmen*], instead of losing and squandering ourselves in the bustle of that which is of today. Our beenness and our future do not have the character of two periods, one of which is already vacant and the other that first has to be occupied, but that which essences from earlier on is *as* future our own being. Our being-thrown-ahead into the future is the future of the beenness: It is the *originally singular and proper time.*

Second Part

The Original Time as the Ground of all Questions Hitherto and the Resumption of the Question-Sequence in Reversed Direction

Time is no side-by-side of periods, among which one cedes the place to another; rather, that which essences temporalizes itself as that which is futural in the manner of reaching over. The proper becoming-character of happening as history lies in the originality of time, not in the flowing off into the past. Time is not a flow indifferent to us. However, time is also not to be understood from the opposite direction, from the coming into being, either; rather, our relation to time in general must become another.

§22. The transformation of our being in its relation to the power of time. Responsibility

We see that beenness, insofar as it reaches over us and comes toward [*zukommt*] us, has future [*Zukunft*]. However, to say that the past has future would be nonsense. The reaching over itself is the future. We do not experience time as an indifferent framework, but as [a] power that carries our own essence, as tradition, which carries us itself ahead in our task. This is also the reason why the human being can miss his task. That would be impossible, if it were not carried ahead of him by virtue of the essence of time.

The illusion can develop that it is ultimately only about another theory of the time-concept. If it were only that, then we would not have much to discuss about that. However, it is rather about an event that we have not invented ourselves; it is about nothing other than the coming up of a transformation of our whole being in its relationship to the power of time, since this transformation depends upon how we ourselves understand the power of time, how we take over the beenness, how we ourselves temporalize time.

Time is no longer the transience that we ascertain or even deplore, nor, conversely, is it the mere coming into being and having-become, indeed cheered as progress.

The radical change concerns the change of our *Dasein*. The question concerning time is not aimed at the ascertainment and decision about facts. The question itself is an intrusion in our actual relationship with time. This intrusion in our time-relationship is the proper sense of the questioning concerning the essence of history. The question arises from a great and long tradition. We may no longer understand ourselves as that which occurs in time; we must experience ourselves as those who determine themselves from the future by essencing from earlier on by reaching out beyond themselves, that is, however: as those who *themselves are time*. We are the temporalizing of time itself.

Insofar as this questioning concerning time does not amount to an empty determination of concepts, all of that which is grounded in the original essence of time—history, *Volk*, human being, language—is also included in this happening of time.

"Who are we ourselves?"—We are included in the happening of education of this university. This is an answer after the manner of decision, as we said earlier. The ground for that has become comprehensible now. It lies in the happening as such. For, now happening is no longer a succession of incidents, but the happening is in itself tradition; and to get involved in the happening means: to take over [*übernehmen*] the tradition [*Überlieferung*], to subordinate oneself to it.

The happening is no flow that makes itself from itself. This is certainly the semblance that belongs to the happening and lets us miss the execution. From here on, we comprehend why we in our questioning had to turn forth the necessity of the corresponding bearing. For, already, the questioning itself is decision-like. Whether we question on, hold out, overcome resistance—all that belongs with the actual questioning: it depends on our decision.

We move no longer in a wrong expectation, for we lurk no longer for any event that could be remembered and repeated. For, the answer to the question concerning history is decision-like too. It does not consist in the proposition that history is thus and thus, and so on. All in all, it is about a kind of answering [*Antworten*] in which we take over an answering and first properly make it into history; it is about an *answering for* [Verantworten].

We are accustomed to understand responsibility [*Verantwortung*] morally or religiously: responsibility before the moral law or before God. The concept "responsibility" is, however, to be understood philosophically as a distinctive kind of answering. Answering is knowingly and deliberately replying. The answering for, however, is never settled. This kind of question can never be replied to [be*antwortet werden*].

§ 23. Rejection of two misunderstandings

From here, it becomes clear how far-reaching and comprehensive is the change of our being that it presents for a long time a transition for us and must be subject to continual misinterpretations. We want to clear up two misunderstandings.

a) No politics of the day position, but
   awakening of an original knowing
One could believe with this decision-like questioning and answering for that it is about [a] simple and practical position with regard to what takes place in our historical moment. However, that does not apply in the sense in which we highlighted any stock of statements. Yet, it is certainly about the awakening of the readiness and the capability for the correct actions, about the formation of the right goals. Precisely for this reason, we insist on an original knowing, on truth in the sense of manifestness, which introduces and binds us in this being. The highest task for this is: to make modes of thinking effective in us, which enables us to put essential things into question and make them comprehensible.

These modes of thinking have a character of concept that is different from the traditional logic. Power and sharpness of logic will not be removed with this, but precisely enhanced, insofar as the concepts are taken out of a false opposition, according to which the concept, that which is thought, is conceived as that which is rational—as distinguished from what is irrational. This distinction leads back to a particular conception of reason, this, in turn, to that of the human being as the rational living being. It is about the overcoming of the conception of the concept as a hull. The consequence is not the dismissal of the concept, but the higher necessity of the conceptual questioning.

Therefore, it would be a misunderstanding to want to find in our remarks an edifying call to take part in any kind of going along; rather, it is about the exposition of concepts, which are the essence of our forthcoming being and thereby concern ourselves.

b) That which is to be found out by questioning
    does not let itself be settled immediately

The other misunderstanding would lie in the expectation that all that which we try to find out by questioning and to bring to an answer here is settled overnight, as it were. This questioning itself does not stand outside of history, but, set in its determination, it reaches beyond day and year; it is not bound to current contingencies.

We have thus attained the ground for the whole realm of the questioning that we have traversed. This ground is time itself as the power, which we pass or do not pass [Trans.: as in passing a test: *die wir bestehen oder nicht bestehen*]; this ground is our *Dasein* as temporality itself. We can no longer say that time may or may not be. We must comprehend that the understanding of being itself is taken *from time*. In the demarcation of becoming against being, being had indeed remained as constancy. From this remaining, the now was conceived as seed of time, so to speak, and future was taken as that which is not yet actual, and past [was taken] as that which is no longer actual. Being was constancy [*Beständigkeit*] and presence; of time, only the fleeting now was always actual.

By having determined now the temporalizing of time from the future and beenness, the present was jumped over as that which disappears. Therefore, a complete transformation of the essence of being becomes apparent here. From here, we must take up the further questions concerning being as history, the being of the human being and the being of language.

Recapitulation

We stand with the attempt to comprehend the essence of history, now taken as *happening*, out of the relationship with time. We discussed three determinations. The first takes history as *past*. We linked up with this determination in our discussion of the second determination. This second conception does not understand history as a mere going by; to be sure, that which is bygone is meant, but this [is meant] in its *having-become*. Yet, also this idea of the becomeness of that which is earlier has a limit, insofar as it mostly considers and must consider the present as the completion of that which has become.

As distinguished from these two determinations, past and becomeness, a third was named, namely, *beenness*. It determines itself as that which essences from earlier on. We asked first of all, how that which essences from earlier on can be circumscribed within an era: That which essences from earlier on of a history is understood as the respective today, as that which is actual today and counts as effective.

This delimitation is threatened by the danger of determining that which is actual today according to that which is unessential because the unessence is not only the mere negation of the essence, but awakens in itself the semblance of essence and thereby misleads and misguides. However, disregarding the fact that the present can also be missed in its essential happening, we cannot at all seize that which essences from earlier on like something extant; it determines itself rather from that for which we decide ourselves as historical beings: from our future, why we place ourselves under command, from that to which end we determine ourselves as that which is forthcoming.

This determination of the future is not subject to choice; nor is it a matter for the theoretical acumen; rather, it comes about from that which essences from earlier on, from tradition [*Überlieferung*]. History hands itself over [*überliefert sich*] into the future, [it] passes forth from there who and what it can be.

Thus, beenness and future are not two periods, not in such a manner that we can slide from one into another, but future and beenness are in themselves united time-powers, the power of the time itself in which we stand. We are only futural as we take over [*übernehmen*] the beenness as tradition.

With this, we have attained a completely different understanding of time in its temporality/temporalizing—and thus the ground from which we can first determine history in its character of happening. Happening is no process, but *tradition*; tradition that reaches over beyond us and reaches through us is to be appropriated only *in such a manner* that we expressly take it over and are in it *itself*. With this, it also becomes comprehensible that our questions concerning the essence of language, human being, concerning ourselves, concerning *Volk* and history—that all these questions are determined *after the manner of decision*. The answering has the character of decision as well. The proposition here is no assessment, no result, which we can repeat or write down for others (we can indeed do that, but that is a mere semblance), but the answering is here always a taking in of that which is said into being and into the decision itself; it is an *answering for* [Verantworten]. Every question and answer [*Antwort*] is responsibility [*Verantwortung*] in a sense that goes beyond that which is moral and religious.

Then we objected to two misunderstandings. On the one hand, we objected to the opinion that it is about an edifying manner of talking about human matters. Surely, it is a matter here rather of grasping the concept of that which the talk is about. Of course, this concept is of another kind than the concepts "tree" and "house." Then, we also objected to the opinion that the answers can be reached overnight and on the ground of a merely verbal understanding.

If we now turn back to the guiding question, then it follows that time in its time-formation (temporalizing) is that power in which alone the happening of our *Dasein* happens in history.

First Chapter

The Historicity of the
Human Being is Experienced from a Transformed
Relationship with Time

One talks much today about the historicity of the human being, and yet one does not come to know the essence of this historicity. One does not comprehend the inner demand that lies in the essence of historicity. This comprehending is only possible in a transformed relationship with time, in an original experience of time. In order to incorporate this transformed time-concept into our *Dasein*, it is necessary to subject our kind of experiencing and understanding of time to a fundamental change, as well as to bring about and to carry through a fundamental experience.

We do not experience time originally in the fact that we look at the clock and ascertain time as a flow that is measurable by the clock, which goes by fast or slowly, nor in the fact that we relate every occurrence that encounters us to its point in time and can date it according to this point in time. We experience time only and properly, if we bring *ourselves in our determination* to the experience.

§ 24. The experience of time through
the experience of our determination

Yet, what does "determination" mean here? In our discussion, we use the expression "determination" in a clearly defined meaning—in a *determinate* meaning, we could have also said, "determinate," no longer comprehended as characterization of an arbitrary thing or concept. We want to give the word "determination" a fuller, more original sense.

The word can be applied at will in everyday usage. We violate it. However, this violence with which philosophy uses words and determines words belongs to its essence. Only in the eyes of the philistine and columnist is word-determination arbitrariness and violence. One does not see that precisely the veiling of language and the random use of words is a much greater violence than a regulation of the meaning of a word arising from inner necessity, whereby it is not about a changing of a word as an empty garment, but about the essence of the matter.

The word "determination," insofar as we talk about *our* determination, has a threefold meaning in [a] *more original* unity and belongingness.

a) Mandate and mission

We do not understand our determination as fixed equipment of our bodily or other condition, nor as the training of ourselves for some purpose, but we understand our determination as the one *for which we determine ourselves*, what we effect for ourselves as our *mandate*. This mandate of our being is our determination—not posited arbitrarily, but our determination, our mandate, our future, in the sense that the mandate is predetermined for us from our *mission*: from that which from earlier on essences in our essence as our essence, although it was obstructed and misinterpreted from earlier on. The mandate as our mission is our determination in an original sense, [it] is the power [*Macht*] of time itself, in which we stand, which empowers [*ermächtigt*] us to our forthcoming, as it bequeaths [*vermacht*] to us the legacy [*Vermächtnis*] of our origin.

By standing in its mission, our *Dasein* experiences its determination and is, in this sense, determined. Determination in this sense means a being-carried-forward in the mission, which comes to meet us as mandate. We see the fundamental constitution of our historical being in this.

However, to what does determination belong?

b) Labor

The second sense, which we ground on the first sense, preserves the determination as we take it over in such a manner that we *create* it. Determinateness in this sense means [a] forming and fitting-together of our entire comportment and our bearing from that which is mission and mandate for us. To effect our determination, to set to work and to bring to work, in each case, according to the sphere of the creating—that means *to labor*.

Labor is not any occupation that we attend to out of calculation, need, pastime, boredom, but labor is here the determination that has become the determinateness of our essence, the form, and the jointure of the execution of our mission and the effecting of our mandate in the respective historical moment.

Labor is the *present* of the historical human being, in such a manner that in labor and through it the work comes to presence and to actuality for us. It follows from this that the historical present determines itself as the historical *moment*. Historical present arises as labor out of mission and mandate, and thus the present arises out of future and beenness.

This shows that the historical present is to be understood as completely different from the current conception, in which the present alone is that which is actual, and past and future are not actual, are that which is not, that which shatters at each now.

The present as *determinateness* of the determination *is* only as crossing from beenness into the future. As crossing, it shows itself in the execution, that is, in the moment. That becomes clearer, insofar as we experience time out of our determination in an original sense: as determination in mandate and mission, as determinateness in the labor that leaps into the mandate and mission.

The mandate determined as labor of a *Volk* in its mission, the determination in this twofold sense, is determination in still a third sense.

c) The being-attuned-through by the mood

We are determined, that is, at all times *attuned-through* by a *mood* [*von einer* Stimmung durchstimmt]. Just as purely as mandate and mission have their determination [*Bestimmtheit*] in labor and only in it, just as labor, on its side, reaches over from beenness into the future, so a fundamental mood [*Grundstimmung*] dominates the whole of mandate, mission, and labor. Determinateness [Be*stimmtheit*] is respectively in an *at*tunement [Ge*stimmtheit*] and a mood [*Stimmung*] that carries it.

One usually conceives moods as [a] certain addition to the proper mental faculties, thinking and willing. They are, as it were, coloring and shading of the experiences [*Erlebnisse*], certain accompanying states toward the cast of mind. In this conception, one misjudges the inner essence of the mood as well as its power. The misunderstanding arises that the so-called strong-willed human beings; the doers, the cold-thinking humans, are exempt from moods; that the mood is something feminine, [that] it is only the business of so-called moody fellows, who continuously go from one mood into another and are always dependent on that.

Here too, we come across the fact that the essence of essentially human distinctions is assessed according to the *un*essence. It is not only the unstable human being who is dependent on moods, but also and precisely the great one; this one is certainly internally fitted and led by great moods; the small human, in contrast, by small moods, which we call humors. The difference between great and small moods lies in the fact that great fundamental moods, the more powerful they are, the more concealed they work. They are all the more powerful, if they make themselves manifest in the own creation of a deed, of a work. A great work is only possible from the fundamental mood, ultimately from the fundamental mood of a *Volk*. Great art too is only possible, if it arises from a fundamental mood. While the great mood is locked in the human being or silent in the great work, the small mood continually displays itself, be it in wretchedness or dull boisterousness.

Moods are no mere infusion in our mental life, but are fundamental events of the power of time in which our *Dasein* is *original*. Moods are that by virtue of which we open or also lock ourselves to beings in the deepest and broadest and most original manner from out of our essence. Our being-determined is at all times attuned in the determinateness of the two named determinations.

This threefold-unified sense of that which we name determination lets us experience mandate and mission, labor and mood, first in their unity, which is in the manner of a happening, [and] with this, time too as original power, which fits [*fügt*] together and in itself determines our being as happening. Time is, thus, experienced as our determination, nothing other than the power-jointure [*Machtgefüge*], the great and sole *joint* [Fuge] of our being as an historical one. It becomes the historical singularity of our self. Thus, time is the fountain of the historical *Volk* and of the individuals in the *Volk*. The unity of this threefold determination is the fundamental-character of the happening.

§25. Original and derived experience of being and of time.
     Temporality and within-timeness.

It is difficult for today's human being to gain from the experience of the thus comprehended determination of being the original essential relationship of the proper being with time, and that is because we have been misguided for a long time by representations of time, according to which it is an empty form into which everything can be packed: Time as *flow*, as *that which goes by* indifferently, along which our everyday runs and thus goes by too—an alienated representation compared with the proper and very own being of the human being. For, time itself takes over and administers and produces. We must above all win the original relationship with time from this experience, if we shall become an historical *Volk* in the distinctive sense.

Here is the opportunity to say that the idea of time that is familiar to us (time as empty form, flow and space) is surely not false. It has rather its own truth and necessity; it does belong after all essentially to our properly historical-temporal being. Yes, this representation that is familiar to us arises from the original temporality itself. *How* the origin of the time that is familiar to us comes to pass from the original [one] cannot be presented here, nor why the familiar time-concept could have and had to gain dominance first and for a long time in the history of the human being.

Nor can we enter into the question of why and in which way it happens that the most essential, deepest, and broadest concept of our understanding, activity, and thinking, the concept of being, is created from a certain idea of time. Being means, namely, constant presence, οὐσία. Why precisely does time, which we are otherwise in the habit of placing together with space, present the realm of origin for the highest concept, for the comprehending of being? From the beginning to the present, the mysterious inner connection has worked in philosophy between the power of time and the respective understanding of being, the respective dominance of a concept of being. Because this connection subsists, therefore, the talk is about "being and time." This is no arbitrary title for any book, but the innermost and most concealed question of our philosophy on the whole and, with this, of its determination, of its mission, of its mandate and of its labor.

If, on the other hand, a complete change of the familiar time-repre-sentation intrudes into our mind and our position toward time produces a revolution (time, not as mere flow, framework for succession of inci-dents), then in this change, our understanding and comprehension of our position toward being must change as well. This change toward which we are heading can only be compared to the change at the begin-ning of the intellectual history of the western human being in general.

Our era is still attached far too much to customary modes of think-ing and ancient ideas for the individual to have a foreboding of this rev-olutionary change. In this peculiar situation of the crossing, in which that which is coming oppresses us and that which is obsolete depresses us, there remains always only: relentlessly to dismantle and to destroy that which is hitherto and to make effective the restlessness of that which is coming.

In the question concerning the being of the human being, concern-ing the being of the *Volk*, the being of history, all things that are wor-thy of question have their roots ultimately in the worthiness of ques-tion of the concept "being in general" and our existing position toward being as time.

We have tried to make time visible as fundamental power of our *Dasein*. With this, it is already indicated that time is characteristic of the human being and belongs to him alone, that, therefore, time—belonging to the human subject—is, accordingly, something subjec-tive. According to the current determination, which we experience as our own happening, the occurrences on the earth, in plants or animals are certainly *flows* and *processes* in the framework of time, but stones, animals, plants are themselves not temporal in the original sense as we ourselves. They take over no mandate, [they] do not submit themselves to a mission so that precisely this submitting oneself, the undertaking, is to constitute their way of being. To be sure, animal and plant do not labor, not because they are carefree, but because they cannot labor. Even the horse that pulls the wagon does not labor; it is only hitched up to an event-of-labor of the human being. The machine does not labor either. That it labors is a misinterpretation of the nineteenth century.

This misinterpretation of labor goes so far that physics has taken up the concept "labor" as a concept of physics. Because labor was granted to the machine, then conversely the human being as laborer was degraded into a machine—a conception that is most deeply connected with a position toward history and toward time in the sense of the unessence of historical being.

Stone, plant, animal are reckonable *in* time, but are not temporal in the sense that their own being shows itself in that. We want to discuss in the following to what extent there is an essential distinction between the historical temporality of the human being and the mere occurrence of animal and plant in time. We want to ask, then, what can it mean that time is something merely subjective, insofar as it is appointed as the sustaining power of being to the human being alone.

Recapitulation

We tried to determine the essence of history and of historical being through the evidence that the *happening* as such is grounded in time, and to what extent. The familiar representation of the time-character is not meant with this, however, but time in the original sense, which is important for us to experience originally. The representation of time that is familiar to us is flow, succession of the now. It is legitimate, insofar as the historical happening is included in a chronology in time and is dated with this.

Originally, this representation was obtained in a natural experience, a temporal experience of things with the purpose of measuring time in the alternation of day and night. The time-conception was, at the same time, oriented to the rising and setting of the sun, which follows its orbit in the heavens. For this reason, time was equated with the heavens. *Chronos* was the god who dominated the flow of things. This mythologically true idea has denatured itself in the course of history and changed into the empty concept of physics, which encounters us as *t* (*tempus*). Time is now that which we ascertain as Central European standard time.

This representation is not false; it is even in itself necessary, but it does not capture the essence of temporality. This arises from the original time, the one in which we experience in what we established as *determination* of our being.

It was this one threefold determination: being-determined, determinateness, attunement [*Bestimmtsein, Bestimmtheit, Gestimmtsein*]. Being-determined in a historical sense happens in the mission, which by reaching over us and by reaching through us, approaches us as mandate, which we cannot rationally calculate and reasonably set up, but that has its peculiar objectivity in the origin of historical being itself. Mandate and mission, future and beenness are an original power that is connected in itself, which closed in itself determines presentness and dominates our being as historical; we characterize it as labor of the human being—labor, not as arbitrary occupation, but as the execution of the forming of and disposing over that which poses itself as task to us in work in our historical *Dasein.*

Mandate, mission, and labor are as this unifying power at the same time the power of the attunement that carries us. Mood is thereby not some experience that only accompanies our other mental bearing, but mood is the fundamental power of our *Dasein*, by virtue of which we are transposed in a distinctive manner into that which is.

With this experiencing determination of being-determined, of determinateness and of being-attuned we are capable of experiencing temporality in its original essence. The familiar idea of time is not, however, eliminated in doing so; rather, it is only from the original time [that it] can be comprehended how it could come to the familiar time-concept. The concept of temporality itself not only determines the idea of historical being, but, in general, the idea of what being, nonbeing, and becoming mean. Time is the leading realm within which we understand being. Insofar as the time-concept changes in history, the concept of being and our fundamental position on beings will alter as well.

In the threefold meaning of *determination,* we experience our being as *temporality.* The power of time fills and circumscribes the essence of our being. From now on, we name this being [*Seiende*], who we ourselves are, the *Dasein* of the human being. We use the word "*Dasein*" in a limited and emphasized sense. Plants and animals are as well, but their being is not *Dasein*, but living. Numbers and geometrical figures are as well, but as mere subsistences. Earth and stone are as well, but merely present-at-hand. Human beings are also, but we name their being as an historical one *Dasein.*

The thus articulated word use is seemingly arbitrary, but it arises from an inner necessity, from an inner unfolding of the matter itself. Because *Dasein* is born by the power of time, born, directed and led, therefore, human being is, as temporal, historical; and, insofar as temporality is that which is distinctive in the essence of the human being, happening as history is the distinctive manner of being of the human being. With this, our earlier thesis is proven that history is the distinctive manner of being of the human being.

Because the human being as temporal is historical in the ground of his essence, therefore, the human being is also unhistorical, that is, driven around in the unessence of the unhistory. In nature, there is neither historicity nor unhistoricity, but it is without history, not dependent on the happening. Nature is without history because it is atemporal. That does not contradict the fact that natural processes are measurable and ascertainable by time. Nature, insofar as it is measurable by time, is in a certain manner in time. We have to distinguish strictly, linguistically and conceptually, between the *being-in-time* of something and the *being-temporal*, which befits only the human being. We name this being-in-time, being-measurable by time, *within-timeness*. We characterize as temporality purely and simply that temporality, according to which time is a power of the essence of the human being.

What is determinable by within-timeness, what is measurable and determinable by the clock, does not need to be temporal. What, in contrast, is temporal, like the human being, can also be within-timely. Human happening *can* be determined by time. We can indicate the date of birth and death of the human being; we can determine them temporally. Nature is within-timely. (Numbers are not in time. The numerical proportion is not measurable and determined by time.) The atemporality of nature comprises ahistoricality in itself, which does not exclude the fact that nature in a certain sense can enter into history, for example, the landscape is site and abode of an historical process; however, it is not for this reason temporal in the sense in which the human being is temporal.

Time as temporality is reserved for the being of the human being as his power. Thus, our question, the question concerning the human being, is from the start the question concerning temporality.

The context traversed by us until now has its beginning with the question of *what* is language and *how* it is. We are trying now to trace back the reverse direction in the sequence of the questions, thereby always retaining in view the temporality of the being of the human being. However, in doing so, we will not strictly keep to the sequence, but [we will] try to see the individual stages in a unified manner, simultaneously, as it were, in order to comprehend, then, language as language. With this retrograde consideration, the essence of temporality will be unveiled more and more as well.

§ 26. Discussion of the concern that time becomes something subjective through the newly won determination

We begin this coherent interpretation with the discussion of an obvious concern that has to do with the whole question concerning the essence of the human being. The concern was already suggested and has now even increased. Because of the one-sided assignment of time to the *Dasein* of the human being and of atemporality to all that is nonhuman, time is assigned to the subject and with this reduced to something merely subjective. With this, time is transferred in the realm of the mental experiences [*Erlebnisse*], to the interior of the human being, to the subject, and is thereby denied of the object, of nature.

This concern presupposes that the human being is a subject and his being, accordingly, subsists in his subjectivity. For, only in this case can time be explained as something subjective on the ground of the assignment to the human being.

It has to be asked: Does the being of the human being let itself be determined by being-subject as distinguished from object? What about the today still familiar leading characterization of the human being as subject?

One could now object that for the refutation of the assignment of time to the subject made by us, [of] the subjectifying of time, it is not necessary to go into the lengthy question concerning the subject-character of the human being. The fact should suffice that natural science speaks of and seeks to investigate the sense of time of animals, for example, of the ants or bees. Hereby, surprising results were indeed unearthed. If, therefore, animals have a sense of time, if their life process not only elapses in time, but that which is alive itself has a sense for time and directs itself according to time and is thus determined by time, then time as *temporality* is no distinctive determination of the human being and, therefore, [is] not reserved for the human being.

a) Do animals have a sense of time?

What about this sense of time in animals? The fact that biology engages in investigations about that does not yet prove that animals have a sense of time and stand in the power of time. Certainly, the fact subsists that birds begin nesting and incubating at a certain time, that swallows assemble at a certain time and fly south. However, do birds need to know about time for this or only even have to have a sense for time as such as well?

This is not necessary. It suffices that animals in their behavior stand under particular influences of certain conditions of the earth, of the atmosphere and the weather. The fact that *we* expressly experience these conditions as belonging to a determinate season does not yet prove a similar relationship with the *animals*, which move in this time in this and that way. What is wonderful is not that animals have a sense of time, but that *without* a time-relationship they are in an entirely *immediate manner* tied into the general happening of nature and with this secure for themselves a certain field, a kind of being to which the human being is not entitled.

The position of the sun, the distribution of light that is connected with that, the degree of cooling, the condition of the plant and animal world and other cosmic relationships perhaps concealed from us, characterize the condition of the earth in autumn, which *we* determine as season in the chronological order and incorporate in it. These incidents, the changes in the atmosphere, have nothing to do with time as such. It is not surprising that animals have a sense of time, but what is surprising is the frivolity of the human being who is not inclined to make understandable to himself that which is so different and particular to the animal and plant life.

It is not proven that animals *have* such a sense and a relationship with time through investigations on the sense of time of animals. The sense of time is no scientific result, but it is presupposed before all investigation with a *fore-grasping metaphysical assertion* on grounds of an uncritically assumed correspondence of animal being with the human being.

Yet, a metaphysical assertion is also our disputation of the sense of time in animals. How is this metaphysical assertion grounded each time? In biology, it is not grounded. However, the ground for our dispute lies in the fact that animals cannot talk, that they have no language. If animals were capable of speech, then they would have to have a relationship with time, then they would have to be temporal in their lives, insofar as a reciprocal relationship between language and time subsists. What thus looks like a sense of time in animals must be explained in another manner.

One could reply that animals could still also be capable of speech, that they could have another language, a language that human beings do not understand. Animals do make themselves understood. However, does the essence of a language in general lie in making oneself understood, and secondly, do animals make themselves understood about something, if they make signs, beckoning and warning tones? The questions are answered in the negative.

The peculiarity of the proper essence of the animal may not be destroyed by a hasty assimilation to what is human. The comparison of human being with animal being is misleading as long as limits are not set between how we interpret the animal and that which is the animal's very own. However, the line can be set only if the being of the human being is in a sufficient manner experienced originally beforehand and conceptualized in his own essence. Only in this manner is the possibility created of releasing animal and plant being as what is merely living and of accepting it in its own wonderfulness.

We cannot, therefore, leave unsettled the question concerning the subject-character of the human being.

b) The question concerning the subject-character of the human being

Should it become apparent that the characterization of the human being as subject is misplaced from the ground up, then the concern about the subjectification of time as senseless must become invalid.

Why can the concern persevere? Because to us "subjective" means: referred and limited to the isolated subject, grown out of the individual isolated subject, experiencing the justification in that alone, not derived from the object. If time, therefore, belongs exclusively to the human being and, accordingly, to the subject, then this means: It is not objective, not taken from the object; it is, consequently, mere semblance. If it is only this, then also the power of history is to be denied. How could time be the power of history, if it is supposed to be only in the subject?

The question concerning the subjectivity of time is decisive for the whole. That which is subjective in the familiar idea is that which is I-like, I-related, I-originated. The I of the human being is the subject, *subiectum*, υποκείμενον that which underlies [*das Unterliegende*], the support [*die Unterlage*], over which something else is erected, as it were. The word υποκείμενον has grown out of Greek philosophy and is only understandable from the concept of being arisen from and was worked out in Greek philosophy. The concept of the υποκείμενον itself participates essentially in this working out of the concept of being.

For the Greeks, "being" ["*Sein*"] means as much as *constant presence*. Constancy and present, however, are time-characters. Being [*Seiend*] is for the Greeks that which perseveres, that which is persevering in the extant things, which maintains itself in the change in the state of things (for example, becoming larger or smaller), in the change of circumstances.

All saying must reach through this that maintains itself, that is *properly a being*, if it wants to assert something about being, *what* it is and *how* it is. The being-thus-and-thus of the state is, insofar as it is determined in the saying, *predicate*, that *through which* something is asserted. And the υποκείμενον, *subiectum*, is that *about which* the predicate asserts something. These harmless statements of grammar are laden through and through with the metaphysics of the Greeks.

υποκείμενον has already with Aristotle a characteristic double sense, which is not coincidental for the Greeks. It means, on one hand, the respective thing itself as that which is constantly persevering in the change of its qualities—therefore, a determination of the *being of the thing*s themselves; υποκείμενον has here an ontological meaning, meaning the proper being of the thing. On the other hand, however, υποκείμενον means that about which the proposition, the λόγος, asserts; that which is the foundation for the predicate in the asserting. υποκείμενον has here, therefore, logical meaning, refers to the λόγος. Both these meanings do not need to coincide. Both, however, *can* go together. The Greeks grasped, for one, all being as that which presences, and, at the same time, the statement, λόγος, is the original form and the trial of this being.

At the beginning of the lecture, we emphasized that the fundamental-character of traditional grammar is derived from Greek logic. Now it becomes clearer what that means. Language was taken by the dominating grammar as propositional discourse-complex in which the things are spoken about in their mere being-present-at-hand.

α) The modern change of meaning of "subject" and "object."
  The threefold detachment of the human being

In the Middle Ages, "subject" had the meaning of *thing that is in itself present-at-hand*. A subject, something that lies at the basis, was a house, a tree, a stone and so on. The Middle Ages also already knows an *obiectum* as that which lies opposite, that which stands opposite, the object [*das Entgegenliegende, Entgegenstehende, den Gegenstand*], and that is in the original sense as that which stands opposite [*entgegensteht*] me, insofar as I place it before me, place it opposite me, *represent* it [*es vor mich stelle, mir entgegenstelle, es* vorstelle]. *Obiectum* is that which is represented. If I imagine, for example, a golden mountain, then that is an *obiectum*. The object [*Objekt*] is that which is thought, imagined, by me, that which properly is merely subjective, as we say today—while that in itself present-at-hand house is exactly the other way round called "object" by us.

The meaning of both concepts "subject" and "object" has completely converted into their opposite. This conversion can be traced in history. It is not, at the same time, about the indifferent change in the meaning of any word, but behind it stands the great shift of ancient being into the medieval and into the current being of the human being.

We saw that the origin of the concept υποκείμενον stands in connection with the fundamental question concerning being. This question concerning being is, according to Aristotle, the task of philosophy, of philosophy in the first place, πρώτη φιλοσοφία, of that which one later called metaphysics. Insofar as in the turning away from ancient and medieval *Dasein* a change took place in the thinking and questioning of being, this had to take place also in metaphysics, in the *prima philosophia*. For this reason, the title of the writing in which the fundamental change took place within philosophy reads "*Meditationes de prima philosophia*—Meditations on first philosophy," appearing in 1641, whose author is Descartes, whom one commonly regards as the founder of modern philosophy.

However, Descartes is dependent, that is, he bears that which is earlier in himself as well and grapples with traditional thinking. That which is earlier in medieval philosophy is conveyed to him through Suárez. Descartes has not been the first to bring about the modern position. The new endeavors have already been awakened before his time in the most diverse areas. Their development carried itself out as a *liberation* from the previous bonds; a reflection on the human being's own powers, the *capacities* of the human being, went, of course, along with it.

This liberation came about in three main areas:

1. It came about in the detachment from the supernatural life order of the Christian church and the authority of the dogmas; in the countermove, one resorted to discovery as well as to the conquest and domination of the world. Here lies the origin of technology, which is more than the domination of tools and of machines, which has its fundamental meaning rather in an altered world-position of the human being.
2. The liberation came about in the detachment of the human being from the bonds of organically [*lebensmäßig*] grown nature. Nature is given a new interpretation as that which is mechanical. The body becomes mere machine, next to which the spirit rules.
3. The liberation came about in the detachment of the human being from the community, from the original orders. It came about, however, not in the direction toward chaos; rather, the human being as an individual conscious of himself becomes the starting point and element of the new order, which receives the character of *society*, that is, of an association. Here is the origin of the new concept of the State (social contract).

The effective powers of this threefold detachment undergo within modern metaphysics the proper metaphysical grounding and expansion. With the course of this change, we can comprehend the shift of the concept "subject"—from that which is permanent in things to that which is I-like—and of the concept "object"—from that which is represented to the objective being of things.

Recapitulation
We determined the essence of human being as temporality and, accordingly, as historicity. We characterized this human being as Dasein. Through language, the *Dasein* of the human being is distinguished from the being of animals as *life*, from the being of the number as *subsistence,* and from the being of lifeless nature as *present-at-hand flow.*

If we comprehend human being as temporality, then this being-temporal of the human being is not understood in the customary sense, that is, [as] measurable by time. Nature is temporal in this usual sense as well; and even that which is atemporal, the number too, is encountered in time. To be sure, that which is temporal in the proper sense (the being of the human being) as well as that which is atemporal (the being of nature) can be measured by time, [can] be *within-timely*, whereby time is here only the framework, but not the power that determines the proper being of the human being. On the ground of this application of temporality as the original essence of the human being, we have found the foundation for a retrospective understanding of that which we have gone through in the previous lessons. We tried to comprehend this uniformly from the ground of human being.

We then discussed the objection that arises from our determination of temporality: If time itself is transposed into the subject, then it is *subjectified*, but entirely withdrawn from the *objective* realm with this. To that, we replied: to be sure, the animal's comportment is in a certain sense determined by time. However, there is no reason to conclude from the given facts of animal being that animals have a relationship with time. These given facts can also be explained without the sense of time, as perhaps by the influence of light, of the warmth or of other cosmic conditions.

The impossibility of the assumption that animals have a sense for time in the same sense as the human being emerges from the impossibility of the idea that animals, if they were to have time, could also lose time. Yet, human being [*das menschliche Sein*] alone has time or has no time, the human being alone loses time. The animal, however, cannot lose time, because it does not have time. From this, the reduction of time to the human being as subject cannot to be refuted.

On the other hand, however, we may not take the objection too lightly, since it implies a certain conception of the human being: the human being as being-subject. Because here the matter is about a fundamental conception of the human being, we must confront it. What does it mean that the human being is subject? What does "subject" mean? How does it come to this application of being human?

The origin is contained in the υποκείμενον and has arisen from Greek philosophy in order to bring the essence of being and the comprehension of beings to understanding —υποκείμενον is that which is as constant presence. In the Middle Ages, υποκείμενον was captured in a certain form, as *subiectum*, as the extant-present-at-hand thing. Obiectum was the counter-concept, that which is represented, thrust against, merely "subjective," merely thought, imagined by the human being—wherein the inverting of the word already paves the way.

How and along which way did it come to this turning around of the fundamental concepts of philosophy, and what does it mean? The inversion comes about in connection with the turning around of western *Dasein* as a whole to modern *Dasein*. This change is to be determined as liberation of the human being from tradition and the structure of the church and of the dogma, as liberation from the bounds of the organically grown nature and as liberation from the community. This liberation is—now understood in the positive sense—to be determined from the depending-on-oneself of the human being by virtue of his own reason and reckoning.

β) The new metaphysical fundamental position of the human being in Descartes' prima philosophia

Within this change, a change also comes about in philosophy in its fundamental position, in metaphysics, therefore, in the questions that antiquity determines as *prima philosophia*, in the question concerning being. Descartes with his "*Meditationes de prima philosophia*" takes part essentially in this change. For, Descartes had first drawn into doubt and placed in question all of the familiar knowledge, all traditional, conventional knowledge, in the sense of the indicated change of the modern spirit—not in order to destroy simply all knowledge, but in order to bring it through detachment from conventional human knowledge and being to a basis and ground laid down by the human being himself.

Descartes drives the doubting of all knowledge up to where he comes across something indubitable, which shall yield the foundation for the new building to come, a *fundamentum inconcussum*, an unshakable foundation, a support for all knowing, something constant, permanent, a *subiectum*.

Along which way does Descartes find this human *subiectum*? How does it present itself as one that is indubitable and constantly present-at-hand? He seeks a first and ultimate certainty and only this. It is indifferent to him which state of affairs proves itself as certain as this support, what satisfies this indubitable certainty—if only something shows itself that satisfies this demand. For Descartes, that which is clearly and distinctly grasped (*clare et distincte perceptum est*) in the sense of the mathematical definition of a mathematical concept is *certain*.

A specific certainty is thought of, a specific idea is key in the search for the foundation. Along this guide-rope, Descartes keeps to the way [on] which he draws into doubt all knowledge of all possible realms and places [it] aside as uncertain, as that which cannot be relied on. If we doubt everything, only the doubting itself finally remains. However, as long as I doubt, I cannot draw the existence [*das Vorhandensein*] of doubt into doubt. Doubting, however, is a manner of thinking, a manner of comportment of consciousness. Thinking is only if I am. I think, I doubt, therefore, I am. This my being, the being of the I, is indubitable, [it] is that which still holds itself out as being in all doubting, [it is] that which is constantly present. "The: *I think* must *be able* to accompany all my representations" (Kant, *Kritik der reinen Vernunft*, B131). The I is that which is constantly present, that which suffices for what is sought for, a *subiectum*; the I is subject.

The I is not, however, an arbitrary *subiectum*, but that fundamental certainty from which all future knowledge is erected. So, this *subiectum*, the I, becomes a distinctive subject. The *subiectum* is now synonymous with I. Each subject is then subject only if it is I. The I comes into the status of the subject. The I-like, that which belongs to the I, is, with this, that which is subjective.

This I as the *indubitable foundation* is for modern thinking as a whole that tribunal from which it is decided whether and in what respect that which is represented, the *object*, is such that it satisfies the requirement of certainty, to which extent that which is represented is a being, an actual object. In this way, the object comes into the role of that which lies opposite the subject, of that which is alien, of the other, of that which is present-at-hand of nature in the broadest sense. Everything that belongs in the realm of beings determined by the I, of that which is after the manner of consciousness, of the mental, experience-like [*Erlebnishaften*], is subjective; all sensations, for example, colors and tones, are subjective, belong in the realm of the subject.

With this, the entire reversal and the turning around of the fundamental words into their counter-meaning is pointed out.

c) The modern determination of human being as being-thing
    in the sense of the mere being-present-at-hand

[What is] much more important than this proof now is the reply to the question which conception and which circumscription of human being takes place by the fact that the I comes into the role of the *subiectum*. In the characterization of the human I as subject, the ancient concept of the ὑποκείμενον, of being as constant presence, becomes visible, read off from the being of the present-at-hand and immediately given things. In this characterization, being-human is determined by being-thing in the sense of mere *being-present-at-hand*.

Insofar as being-I is the most original certainty for this mode of thinking, there is intentionally no longer an asking about the being of the I on the ground of this most original certainty. This foundation obtains such power that it is not only experienced as immediately certain, but also that the being of the *object* is acknowledged only insofar as it satisfies the requirement of certainty. The task arises of comprehending the being of objects as a being of the I. This task occupies philosophy up to Hegel. He declares in his phenomenology that it is the task of philosophy to comprehend substance, that which is in itself the objective that is present-at-hand, as the subject, to determine things as I and I as thing.

For this mode of thinking that became self-evident and, for us, worn out, every question concerning the peculiar mode of being of the human being is kept aside. If, therefore, Descartes' procedure on the ground of the fundamental doubt looks very radical, and is also passed off as this, then in the end it becomes apparent that Descartes did not recognize the true critical question in what is decisive, namely, the one whether it is possible to conceive the being of the human being as being-subject and to conceptually determine it by this mode of being. Thus, it comes about that the proper being of the human being is experienced in the I that is dependent on itself and encapsulated in an empty being. For this reason, the question of how this I that is locked in itself comes into a relationship with the not-I, with the object, also arises.

This formulation of the question, which still dominates today, rests on an impossible foundation. The consequences of the thus characterized priority of the I as a subject in the conception and determination of being-human let themselves be pursued in the form of becoming shallow through the whole nineteenth century up to current times. Liberalism has its roots in this conception of the human being. The fight against liberalism moves in worn out phrases, instead of in [a] genuine revolution of the whole of being and knowledge. For this reason, one does not need to wonder that the relapses are most frequent where one shouts the loudest. Our everyday mode of thinking is still stuck through and through in the foundations of liberalism that have not been overcome.

The concern that time becomes something subjective in our conception also stems from here. As long as one thinks of the human being as subject (and with this comprehends time as I-like), the concern is, of course, grounded. However, our elaboration of being human avoids the designation of the human being as an isolated I and has as goal an originally new experience of the being of the human being.

The objection that we would make time something subjective becomes senseless because the thinking of temporality shakes up and blasts precisely the conception of the human being as I from the ground up. This happens insofar as temporality *un*binds [ent*schränkt*] the binding [*die* Be*schränkung*] of the human being to an isolated subject. For, the rightly comprehended and original temporality can no longer give rise to the representation of the human being as isolated subject. This change is difficult and [is] our task for a long time.

There is nothing more familiar than the idea of the human being as an individual who is found among others, among his equals, and among things. With this, the bounds of the human being run along the surface of his skin; it is, as it were, the boundary of that which is without and that which is within. Heart, brain, diaphragm are within as the seat of that which is mental, of the experiences [*Erlebnisse*]. These experiences [*Erlebnisse*] take place. The human being has experiences [*Erlebnisse*], just as he has legs and a stomach. He is subject to experiences [*Erlebnisse*], runs around, and is, at the same time, subject to the most different influences and effects, to which he reacts for his part. One can now illustrate this idea in a more intellectual manner by raising the I into personality or lowering it to a "degenerated subject."

The seemingly natural mode of experience is decisive, by virtue of which living beings endowed with reason encounter us. This mode of experience has a certain legitimacy, but it is questionable whether it can be *decisive*, if the *kind of essence* of the human being has to be found. Our examination has already shown that this mode of experience does not suffice.

Second Chapter

The Experience of the Essence of the Human Being from His Determination

§ 27. The in-one-another of mood, labor, mission, and mandate

The experience of being-human in and from its *determination* in a three-fold sense is to be raised to the light more sharply in its rendering, to be made conceptually graspable and effective for the acting understanding.

a) Mood. The relationship of mood and body
Our determination [*Bestimmung*] in a threefold sense is attuned [*gestimmt*], carried by a respective mood [*Stimmung*], be it the one of being-repressed or of being-elevated and being-elated. As fundamental moods, we also have the harmony with all things, desolation, boredom and emptiness or the fulfilled profound emotion and confidence.

We take these moods customarily as characteristics and announcing signs of our mental condition, as proof of how it looks in the interior of an individual subject, of how he feels. We take moods as experiences [*Erlebnisse*] in the subject that boil up, simmer, and evaporate, like the water in a cooking pot, depending on the degree of heat. We misinterpret mood, because we do not want to see that precisely mood transposes us into the whole of beings, that each time it first circumscribes the sphere of beings beforehand, as it discloses [*eröffnet*] and keeps open [*offenhält*] the sphere of beings.

We take, for example, the mood of annoyance: The annoyed one, he may have the most penetrating glance and understanding, [but] may hear and see nothing; the annoyance obstructs all things to him, they are draped and dejected to him. Conversely, joy makes all things bright, simple and clear, it lets us see things in a mode in which we do not otherwise experience them. Yet, also in the indifferent living on, the mood is not perchance lacking, but we are in the being-attuned of the indifference.

However, it is not enough here that we take notice of the peculiarities of mood—that we become perhaps blind in certain cases, clear-sighted in others—and, as before, represent the mood to ourselves as situated in the subject. Rather, it is to be comprehended that we are transposed [*versetzt*] by mood and, by virtue of it, into beings and their being, that mood discloses and closes up beings to us. By virtue of mood, we are *exposed* [ausgesetzt] into the being [*das Sein*] that oppresses or elevates us. We are not first isolated in an I that is curled up in itself, that subsequently comes into a relationship with things, but we are each time already in a mood, which exposes us beforehand into beings themselves. We ourselves dwindle in such exposedness into the thereby manifest being [*Sein*].

Precisely that which we like to characterize as that which is inner, and [which we] transfer into the mind, is not in there anywhere, like in a stomach, but it is outside, and we are outside by virtue of it in each case. Mood determines us in such a manner that we stand essentially in the exposedness.

That which is visible and graspable of ourselves from the outside, the body, which we sense from inside, seems to be the properly main thing in the present-at-hand human being. With its help, we stand with both legs firmly on the ground. The body, not the dangling in exposedness through mood, counts thus as supporting ground. However, what do legs, body and other extremities mean here? If we were to have a dozen or more legs, we would not then stand firmer on the ground. We would not stand at all, if this standing were not attuned-through by moods, by virtue of which earth, ground; in short: nature first bears, preserves and threatens us.

What we ascertain as body is not in itself present-at-hand, [it] is not that which is original of *Dasein*, but it is, as it were, suspended from the power of the moods. Only a perverted thinking that regards that which is palpable as that which is gets into trouble here: It takes mood as bustle of a body that is in itself present-at-hand.

In the affirmation of the body's being-born-by mood, the body does not become fancifully spiritualized, but precisely by virtue of the interwovenness in mood, corporeality has for us that which is oppressive and relaxing, that which is confusing or preserving. We know the connection always only one-sidedly as dependence of the fleeting moods on the constancy of the body. We say, for example, "A stomachache puts a damper on the mood," and we talk of "upset stomach"; however, with this, we do not think that a mood can cause a stomachache. What is illness? Illness is not the disturbance of a biological process, but an historical happening of the human being, something that is grounded among other things in being-attuned.

Thus, blood and bloodline can also essentially determine the human being only when it is determined by moods, never from itself alone. The call of the blood comes from the fundamental mood of the human being. It does not hover by itself, but belongs also with the unity of the mood. To that also belongs the spirituality of our *Dasein*, which happens as labor.

b) Labor

We characterized labor as the present. That shall not mean that labor is that which is respectively present at the time. Labor, according to its spirituality, is present, insofar as it transposes our being in the binding appropriate to work, in the liberation of beings themselves. (We remind ourselves that we have made the following assignment: Mandate—future; mission—beenness; labor—present, respectively, moment.) In labor and through it beings first become manifest to us in their determinate regions, and as laborer the human being is transported into the manifestness of beings and their jointure. This transporting is nothing supplementary, grafted onto the I, but this transporting belongs to the essence of our being. This transportedness into things belongs to our constitution.

For that reason, one is correct in saying that unemployment is not only the privation of a merit, but it is a mental shattering—not because the lack of labor thrusts the human being back to the individualized isolated I, but because the lack of labor leaves empty the being-transported into things. Because labor carries out the relation to beings, therefore unemployment is an emptying of this relation to being. The relation remains, to be sure, but it is unfulfilled. This unfulfilled relation is the ground of the desolation of the one who is without labor. In this desolation, the relation of the human being to the whole of beings is as lively as ever, but as *pain*. Therefore, unemployment is impotent being-exposed.

Labor is correspondingly a transporting into the jointures and forms of the beings that surround us.

That is why the enjoyment of one's labor is so important. It is not a mood that only accompanies our labor; it is no addition to labor, but joy as fundamental mood is the ground of genuine labor, which in its execution first makes human beings capable of existence.

In labor as the present [*Gegenwart*] in the sense of making-present [*Gegenwärtigung*], the making-presence [*Anwesendmachen*] of beings happens. Labor is the present in the original sense, in that we attend toward [*entgegenwarten*] beings and thus let them come over us in their historicity, in that we submit ourselves to their superior strength and administer them in the great mood of the battle, of astonishment and of reverence, and increase it in its greatness.

We can now unfold the essence of labor in its wholeness and fullness just as little as the moods in their great eruptions. What matters here is only to make visible in a first reference the exposedness of *Dasein* by virtue of the attuned transporting into labor, in order to give guidance for the experience of our *Dasein* with this.

c) Mission and mandate

Just as little as mood is only for itself, but always attunes a laboring comportment, just as little is labor a passing condition in the now. Every labor arises from a task and is bound to that which is handed down, determines itself from mandate and mission. *Dasein* is each time already sent ahead of itself and delivered into the tradition [*ausgeliefert in die Überlieferung*] by virtue of them [Trans.: reading *ihrer* as plural]. Beenness as tradition and the future (as that which is forthcoming to us) as task hold *Dasein* fundamentally and always already in an unbinding. Exposed into mood and transported into labor, we are historical. The power of time temporalizes originally and not complementarily the transporting of *Dasein* into the future and beenness.

The being-transported into the present of labor and the extending of *Dasein* into the future and beenness is not understood in the manner of the being-present-at-hand of individual subjects, which are endowed with an interior, around which something is also exterior. Our being subsists in an original exposedness into beings. By virtue of mood, we are from the ground up always already lifted off into the whole of being, so that beings are manifest. This manifestness binds us into beings and grounds an original—determined in this or that way—belongingness to one another in the midst of beings.

Precisely by virtue of mood, the human being is never an individual subject, but he stands always for- or against-one another, in a with-one-another. This is also valid when, as in longing, the other is not yet immediately there. The being-with-one-another of human beings is not in virtue of the fact that there are several human beings, but several human beings can only be in community, because being-human already means: attuned being-with-one-another, which is not lost, if a human being is alone.

The exposedness creates for itself every time its form, its breadth, and its limits through labor, which, according to its essence, transports us into exposedness to the jointure of being liberated for work. Labor is not subsequently, for purposes of a better execution, dependent on the labor of others, but conversely, labor as fundamental comportment of the human being is the ground for the possibility of the being-with-one-another and being-for-one-another. Labor as such, even if it is done by one individual, transports the human being into the being-with-and-for-another. This transporting into the exposedness happens as the human being is set out beyond himself in tradition. The mission itself is in advance withdrawn from arbitrariness and obstinacy.

§28. The blasting of the being-subject through the determination of the Volk

We thus disclose the being of the human being in a manner that we, in comparison with the usual determination of the human being as subject, would have to say: Exposedness, transportedness, tradition, and mandate—through that, the being-subject is blasted, that which is thing-like in a consciousness-box is blasted apart; beings and, with this, first a self are disclosed. Of such a blasting open of the essence of the human *Dasein* we can only speak from the counter-representation of the human being as an isolated and encapsulated I. However, it is erroneous to believe that being-human is encapsulated at first and would have to be subsequently ripped out of this encapsulation.

This kind of being-human lets us first of all comprehend *how* and *who* the being [*das Seiende*] must be to satisfy alone such being [*Sein*].

This being [*Seiende*] is never subject, nor an assembly of several subjects, who by virtue of agreements first ground a community, but the originally united being [*Seiende*] bearing exposedness, transportedness, tradition, and mandate can only be what we call "a *Volk*."

Only in virtue of this being [*Seins*], of the determination, can individuals as well comport and experience themselves as individual. Only on the ground of such an experience can the comportment of the individual be perverted and misinterpreted; misinterpreted as the emptiness of the limited I. On the other hand, individuation in a genuine manner, understood from the original experience of being-human from temporality and, with this, from historical being [*Seins*], is possible and necessary; only, we may not think of the individual according to the idea of the subject. The individuation in solitude can be effective in a unique manner for the whole. Conversely, active taking part does not nearly prove living close ties with the *Volk*; it rather hides egoism. The being of the *Volk* is neither mere occurrence of a population, nor animal-like being, but determination as temporality and historicity.

a) Original manifestness of beings and scientific objectification.
   Contrasting of the animal life with the historical *Dasein*
However, we still have not completely exhausted the essence of the power of time. Yet, it was already indicated in the characterization of exposedness, transporting, tradition, and sending ahead, how through mood and in it, how through truth and in it, how through mission and mandate and in them, beings as a whole and, according to their different realms, are already respectively unlocked and lifted out of concealedness. By virtue of this unconcealedness of beings, they do not stand perhaps like an object opposite a subject; beings are not at all encountered first as ob-ject. This error has established itself, because one always first and only inquired beings insofar as they are and how they are meant and are graspable in science. However, beings are originally manifest in that manner that the human *Dasein*, as attuned and laboring is fitted into the being of nature and of the powers of nature, into the being of the produced works and the effected destinies and situations. Only on the ground of such an original manifestness is such a thing like an objectification of beings possible: the fact that [they] are considered *as* standing-opposite, and experienced and meant *only in this manner*.

However, the being of beings is not exhausted in being-object. Such an error could only arise, indeed, had to originate where from the start things were designated as ob-jects; and this, in turn, presupposed the conception of the human being as subject. Yet, beings in general never originally open themselves up to us in the scientific knowledge of objects, but in the essential moods of labor that vibrate therein and from the historical determination of a *Volk* that determines all of this.

However, the unconcealedness of beings never completely releases them from concealedness. On the contrary: insofar as unconcealedness of beings happens, precisely only their concealedness comes into power. We do not win the today much sought after irrationality by tumbling around in blurred obscurities and dilettantism, but only in that way that the most radical and most rigorous knowing comes up to the limits.

Plants and animals and all life are interwoven in that which is, in a manner, to be sure, that they too are affected by that which is and, in turn, arrange themselves in it, even in the manner of a certain correctness of behavior and of managing that operates like memory and in permanent tracks. However, in all of that, the animal remains ensnared in the—moreover, vague—surrounding field of its behavior. Beings *as* beings do not encounter the animal; beings are neither manifest nor concealed to the animal. What presses in the life sphere of the animal, after that it chases; the animal grabs for, snaps at, and devours it. The animal is this snapping—whereby precisely that at which it snaps never presses against as such a thing at which it snaps, never as a being that the animal fits into being as such. The snapping ensnarement of the animal, of that which is living, is essentially different from the attuned and laboring exposedness of the historical *Dasein* that is transported into being.

b) The happening of history is in itself lore of the disclosedness of
   beings. Historiographical knowledge as degradation of the great
   moments that are disclosive

The happening of history is such a one that is an exposed-transported-extending in itself. That means: That in the midst of which history happens is manifest as such through the happening. It oppresses and threatens, hampers and discloses *as that which is* [als Seiendes]. In other words, the happening is *in itself* lore [*Kunde*]—it announces [*kündet*] beings [*das Seiende*], in which it—dispersed in them—remains fitted. The question, which we first left standing unsolved, now obtains its answer: Lore is not pasted on history from the outside, but happening as exposed-transported is in the manner of announcing, namely, that wherein history is exposed, whither it is transported. And, with this, lore is not some kind of cognizance running alongside what "takes place," but, as what belongs to the extending of that which is historical, it announces the entire happening and the situation of its moment, respectively.

This situation is not the mere storage of circumstances, sometimes one way and sometimes another, but an historical situation each time announces in itself the historical being [*Sein*] as a whole; "announces," that does not mean: gives only knowledge and news, but introduces mandate, mission, and labor. That which is properly historical lies always in the heralding of the great moments and their power for revolution, which gathers the entire happening in it, but not where one commonly seeks out history: in the pacified abating of the moment, an abating and fading away, which one interprets precisely as development, from which the great moments look like interruptions and collapses. In historiographical knowledge, the lore of the happening is mostly degraded into the superficiality and smoothness of the sensible simple-mindedness that stops at nothing because it already knows everything and knows better.

In such a manner, that which is news-like and anecdote-like in history—that which is insignificant and reckonable—gets a green light. And what lies outside of placidity and orderliness—that which is extraordinary, excessive—what each time exceeds that which is usual and that which has strayed-hither is shoved away as that which is merely unreckonable, unclear, and hostile. Yet, the genuine lore [*Kunde*] of history announces [*kündet*] precisely as it sets us before that which is concealed. The mystery of the moment is the lore of that which is overpowering and inevitable. In the mystery, the happening of history has its very own solidity. The simpler the mystery, the more powerful the exposedness in beings and with this of their lockedness.

c) The historical *Dasein* of the human being as the resoluteness toward
   the moment

For this reason, the *Dasein* of the human being as historical can only be properly historical in the resoluteness toward the moment. Resoluteness [*Entschlossenheit*] is not, to be sure, the blind load of a great quantity of so-called will power, but the action that is opened [*aufgeschlossene*] for the mystery and transported into being, to which the possibility of decline, that is, sacrifice, remains continuously near.

For this reason, it is also an erroneous expectation that one could be informed about mandate and mission and be kept abreast, like perhaps, about the weather. The lore of history is given only for him who stands in resoluteness; only he can and may know the inevitability of the historical *Dasein*. However, the unknowing ones, and even those who are drifting around in the unessence of history can, all the same, never release themselves from history and labor. For, even the irresoluteness [*Unentschlossenheit*], the self-shutting [*das sich verschließende*] just-barely-still-staggering-along, is always, because essential, different from the snapping ensnarement of the animal in nature.

Irresoluteness is, as disavowal of the essence of the human-historical *Dasein,* always the affirmation of its unessence. In opposition to this, the animal preserves every time —in its manner—the essence of living. Even in the defection from task and mandate the human being cannot avoid his being; even in decadence must he testify to the fact that whoever he is and how he is, his being and being-possible remain transferred [*übereignet*] to him.

d) Human being as care: Exposedness in beings and delivery over to being. Rejection of the misinterpretation of care: Care as freedom of the historical self-being

With what was now said we point into an even more original depth of the human *Dasein*. Several times already, different kinds of being were contrasted with each other: present-at-hand flow of lifeless things, life of plant and animal, subsistence of the number in the broader sense, *Dasein* as being-human. However, it does not suffice to elucidate the manner of being of the human being in its own constitution, but it is important to see to what extent this being, that we ourselves are, has a relationship to its being.

In contrast, all nonhuman beings are surely not alienated from their own being, for even alienation from being is still a relationship with it. The nonhuman beings are, as distinguished from transferal and alienation, constrained, curled up, dull, compact, and sealed up. These beings do not even relate indifferently to the manner of their being. We, on the other hand, are in such a manner that in this *Are* and *Being* lies:

[we are] transferred and delivered over [*übereignet und überantwortet*] to being, which is at stake insofar as we [are], and as long as we are beings [*Seiende sind*]. And because exposedness and transportedness into being, precisely also [the being] of the beings that we are not, belongs to our being, the delivery over [*Überantwortung*] to being means as much as the transferal [*Übereignung*] to the being of beings as a whole.

This delivery over [*Überantwortung*] turns the historical *Dasein* of the human being into that being that in its determination must answer [*antworten*] to being every time in this way or that way, must answer for [*verantworten*] it. Exposedness in the manifest beings, transportedness into the worked on and worked for [*bearbeitete und erarbeitete*] being of the work and fate in mandate and mission—all of this in unity means at the same time and more originally: delivery over to being. From it and in it every event [*Geschehnis*] of *Dasein* happens [*geschieht*]. This fundamental essence of being human, exposedness into beings and delivery over to being, I called and I call also henceforth "care."

This interpretation of the essence of the human *Dasein* as care has been misinterpreted in all possible directions. The finger-snapping placidity of the philistine believed that the human *Dasein* should not be exclusively declared to be as gloomy as care, for love also belongs to human living. In order to prove that, the unavoidable Goethe was promptly referred to in the publication of the Prussian Academy of the Sciences, in the *Deutschen Literaturzeitung*. Others find that the conception of *Dasein* as care is an expression of an irksome and intimidated "*Weltanschauung*," especially since elsewhere *Angst* is also spoken about; they recommend the "heroic" bearing. Again others, conversely, take offence at the too strong emphasis on that which is after-the-manner-of-practical-engagement and miss the sufficient estimation of the reflective and contemplative human being.

However, all are on the wrong track with their mutually opposing concerns; better, they are not yet at all on the track to understand what is said distinctly enough: that with the characterization of human being as care an accidental affect of the human subject should not be exaggerated and turned forth opposite others, but that care means here exposedness in being, and that means the blasting of all subjectivity. Care is the fundamental constitution of being-human as temporality, from which any mood first becomes first of all possible. Because the human being is exposed in beings, transported into beings and extended as historical being, therefore, he can only be by standing in exposedness, standing for or against it, and thus passing [Trans.: as in passing a test: *besteht*] the being that he is.

This subsisting, standing-out and standing-through [*Bestehen, Aus- und Durchstehen*] of being, to which we are delivered, that standing [*das Stehen*] in beings as such, we call "insistence" ["*Inständigkeit*"]. Human being has its duration as historical, not because of the fact that it is continually present-at-hand like other beings, but in that it endures the exposedness of its being and grounds [it] in resoluteness. Insistence is the manner in which we pass [*bestehen*] our determination each time. Insistence is a character of care, but does not coincide with its full essence. However, because the human being essences toward being in an open relationship of transferal and alienation, the character of the self belongs to human being. The being of *Dasein* as care is the ground of the possibility of the selfhood of human being.

Now it becomes clear why the character of the self does not consist in the reflexivity of the I, of the subject; for it is precisely the blasting of I-ness and of subjectivity by temporality, which delivers *Dasein*, as it were, away from itself to being and thus compels it toward self-being. For this reason, *Dasein*, of course, must be ours, respectively, mine and yours, respectively. If we say: *Dasein* is mine, respectively, then, according to the fundamental blasting of I-ness and subjectivity, it can no longer mean that this *Dasein* is taken back into the individual I and seized by it; rather, "*Dasein* is mine, respectively" means simply that my being is transferred to the with-one-another and for-one-another. I am, therefore, myself only by the fact that I am historically, in the resoluteness toward history. It is no accident that the highest and sharpest individuation of self-being toward the own *Dasein*, respectively, happens in the relationship with death, wherein the broadest exposedness, the hardest transportedness and the deepest extending of the human being in being, and with this the most original expropriation of all I-ness, manifests itself.

Because *Dasein* is care, therefore, it has the essential character of the self; and because *Dasein* has this essential character, therefore, the question concerning the being of the being that we call human being, is not a What-question, but a Who-question. By posing the Who-question to the human being, we ourselves enter the question as a result of the Who-questioning regarding our being as one that is historical.

Care is the fundamental essence of our being. That means: It is about our being. And that means according to the previous: It is about our determination in the threefold sense. Care is in itself care of the determination. Care means: The essence of *Dasein* is of such a kind that, exposed in the manifest beings, it remains transferred to the inevitability of being.

Opened binding in that which is inevitable means freedom. Care is, as such, care of the freedom of the historical self-being. Freedom is not the independence of doing and letting, but carrying through the inevitability of being, taking over the historical being in the knowing will, reforming of the inevitability of being into the dominance of a structured order of a *Volk*. Care of freedom of the historical being [*Seins*] is in itself empowering of the power of the State as the essential-jointure of an historical mission.

e) The State as the historical being of a *Volk*

Because the being of the historical *Dasein* of the human being is grounded in temporality, that is, [in] care, therefore, the State is essentially necessary—the State, not as an abstract, and not [as] derived from a right [that is] invented and relative to a timeless human nature that is in itself, but the State as the law of the essence of historical being, by virtue of whose decree the *Volk* first secures for itself historical duration, that is, the preservation of their mission and the struggle over its mandate. The State is the historical being of the *Volk*.

The *Volk* is neither that spongy and jelly-like sentimentalism, as how it is today offered around often in a prosy manner, nor is the State only the present shut down form of organization, as it were, of a society. The State *is* only insofar and as long as the carrying out of the will of rule happens, which originates from mission and mandate and, conversely, becomes labor and work. The human being, the *Volk*, time, history, being, the State—those are no abstracted concepts as objects for definition exercises, but the essential relationship is always an historical one, however, that means, self-deciding that futurally-has been.

All overcoming of the genuine and non-genuine tradition must [go] in the crucible of the critique of historical resoluteness. That applies last but not least to the title that shall characterize the formation of our historical being, of "socialism." It means no mere changing of the economic mentality; it does not mean a dreary egalitarianism and glorification of that which is inadequate. It does not mean the random pursuit of an aimless common welfare, but it means the care about the standards and the essential-jointure of our historical being, and it wills, therefore, the hierarchy according to occupation and work, it wills the untouchable honor of every labor, it wills the unconditionality of service as the fundamental relationship with the inevitability of being.

The questioning concerning our self-being originates from the essence of historical being as futurality, as care. For, this questioning is, as just we must see now, not the curiosity of the bystander; rather, questioning is in itself care of knowing. Knowing, however, is the labor of carrying through the truth of *Dasein* as one that is grasped and comprehended.

Third Chapter

Being-Human and Language

The question concerning the essence of the human being and its answer have changed for us from the ground up. And that which is decisive here is not the fact that this questioning and answering is merely new or different than what is known; for "old" and "new," those are always only valuations from the perspective of the bustle and boredom of what is of today. From our questioning and answering, it remains essential that they themselves must be comprehended from the being of our historical *Dasein*—from care—that this questioning and answering is only that which it shall be, if it, and as long as it, has the character of our being, the character of insistence, remains insistent, is an insistent questioning that also comprises the questioners.

However, the question "Who is the human being?" had to be asked because we posed the question concerning the essence of language; for every question of the essence is a fore-question. We asked at the start: "Where and how is language at all?" Language is only insofar as the human being is, and it is, accordingly, only in that way as the human being is. However, the manner in which the human being is, is grounded in who he is.

We tried to illuminate the essence of the human *Dasein*, and comprehended the being of the human being as temporality and care, as care of the determination. Now it would only remain that we, as it were, built language into the constitution of human *Dasein* set forth. Language—do we, after all, know what language is? No. We know it so little that language only now with the idea of human *Dasein* becomes worthy of question for us, in the rightly grounded sense becomes questionable. It would be a cheap trick, if we now were to begin, with the help of the gained insight into the constitution of the essence of *Dasein* and of the concepts developed with this, to define the essence of language.

§ 29. Language as the ruling of the world-forming and preserving center of the historical Dasein of the Volk

In the course of our questioning, we said several times that, at the same time, though not explicitly, it is always already a matter of language. In how far was this so?—Insofar as the power of time as temporality constitutes our essence, we are exposed in the manifest beings, and that means at the same time: The being of beings is transferred to us. Being as a whole, as it rules through and rules around us, the ruling wholeness of this whole, is the *world*. World is not an idea of theoretical reason, but world announces [*kündet*] itself in the lore [*Kunde*] of historical being, and this lore is the manifestness of the being of beings in the mystery. In lore, and through it, world rules.

This lore, however, happens in the primal-event of language. In it, the exposedness into beings happens, the delivering over [*Überantwortung*] to being happens. World rules—*is* a being [*ist Seiendes*]. By virtue of language and only by virtue of it. Language does not take place in the encapsulated subject and is then handed around as means of communication among subjects. Language is neither something subjective nor something objective; it does not at all fall in the realm of this groundless distinction. Language is as historical, respectively, nothing other than the event of exposedness entrusted [*überantworteten*] to being into beings as a whole.

The loveliness of the valley and the menace of the mountain and of the raging sea, the sublimity of the stars, the absorption of the plant and the ensnarement of the animal, the calculated speed of machines and the severity of the historical action, the harnessed frenzy of the created work, the cold boldness of the questioning that knows, the hardened sobriety of labor and the discretion of the heart—all that *is* language; wins or loses being only in the event of language. Language is the ruling of the world-forming and preserving center of the historical *Dasein* of the *Volk*. Only where temporality temporalizes itself, does language happen; only where language happens, does temporality temporalize itself.

§ 30. Logic as still not comprehended mandate of the human-historical Dasein: care about the ruling of the world in the event of language

However, why do we ask about the essence of language? Because our *Dasein* is care—the care of determination, its awakening, overtaking, and preservation; because care as care of freedom is the care of knowing and of being-able-to-know about the essence of all beings; because we may not consider the knowing over either the fleeting knowledge of mere facts or as the idle talk that drives along over all things; because knowing can only be grounded and formed, can only be passed on and awakened by the responsible word [*verantwortliche Wort*], that is, by the grown solidity of creational language in the historical labor.

And why do we call this questioning concerning the essence of language "logic"? Because logic deals with λόγος and "λόγος" means talk, that is, language. Because, precisely by the so-called logic, the essence of language was rashly leveled, and superficialized, and misinterpreted, therefore, logic is a still not comprehended mandate of the human-historical *Dasein*. Because this former logic as doctrine of mental acts claimed to hold as highest and authoritative regulation of all determination of being, therefore, this claim must be grasped in a more original manner and [must] be relentlessly renewed from the original concepts of the essence of language.

Logic is for us nothing that an individual could manufacture overnight and bring to the market as [a] text manual. Logic is not, and never is, for the sake of logic. Its questioning happens as the care of knowing about the being of beings, which being comes to power as the ruling of the world happens in language.

§ 31. Poetry as original language

However, such a questioning concerning the essence of language cannot take it up in its unessence; it may not misappropriate this semblance of the essence and misinterpret everything. The essence of language announces itself, not where it is misused and leveled, distorted, and forced into a means of communication, and sunken down into mere expression of a so-called interior. The essence of language essences where it happens as world-forming power, that is, where it in advance preforms and brings into jointure the beings of beings. The original language is the language of poetry.

However, the poet is not he who writes verses about the respective present. Poetry is no soothing for enthused little girls, no charm for the aesthetes, who believe that art is for savoring and licking. True poetry is the language of that being [*Sein*] that was forespoken to us a long time ago already and that we have never before caught up with. For this reason, the language of the poet is never of today, but is always in the manner of having been and futurally. The poet is never contemporary. Contemporary poets, to be sure, can get organized, but they remain nonetheless an absurdity. Poetry, and with it, proper language happens only where the ruling of being is brought into the superior untouchability of the original word.

In order to comprehend this, the Germans, who talk so much today about discipline [*Zucht*] must learn what it means to preserve that which they already possess.

EDITOR'S EPILOGUE

Logic: no "drill for a better or worse method of thought," but the "questioning pacing off abysses of being," no "dried up collection of eternal laws of thought," but "the place of the worthiness of question of the human being"—under this claim stood for Heidegger, the two-hour lecture held in the summer semester of 1934 "*Logic* as the Question Concerning the Essence of Language."

The lecture now at hand as volume 38 of the Collected Edition follows a structure that is conclusive in itself. The introduction first gives a presentation of the traditional scholastic logic and leads to the exposition of the task of a "shaking up" of this logic: The handicap of western logic, its dependency on presence-metaphysics, is made evident and put into question during the entire course of the lecture—with a view to the future determination of the academic subject, but also of the futural being-human in general.

This endeavor is realized in the *first Part* about the essence—that is, fore-questioning concerning language, human being, and history, in order to push forward to the original time as the ground of that which is posed into the question. The *second Part* takes up this questioning anew in a *reversed direction* and concludes consistently with the realm from which the *first Part* took its departure and which, according to what is expounded in the lecture, can no longer be characterized now as an isolated realm: with language. "Logic," to which term Heidegger explicitly holds fast, remains with this the still "not comprehended mandate" of the human-historical *Dasein*: the care about the rule of the world in the event of language.

This lecture is in several respects an unusually interesting document. It presents in an intelligible manner a problematic that is also today still actual—today, since on the one hand, the professorships in logic are predominantly occupied by mathematicians, who here naturally only treat *their*, that is precisely mathematical, therefore, scientific problems, and since, on the other hand, for the philosophers in academia, it remains no more than a introductory course for basic studies. The Heideggerean lecture offers itself in order to think over this constitution of *logic* that is indeed rightly worthy of question: The sober logician would meet with the no less sober Heideggerean thinking. For, though Heidegger was not interested in the academic school discipline *logic,* logic was to him "all the more no undisciplined idle talk about *Weltanschauung*, but sobering work that is bound in the genuine impulse and in essential need."

This lecture is also interesting as an important milestone in the course of Heidegger's development from the fundamental-ontological toward the being-historical phase. And this lecture is in addition important for an adequate understanding of Heidegger's situation at the university shortly after the resignation from the rectorship. Much of that which was written somewhat hastily about Heidegger's national-socialist engagement will be revised on the basis of this lecture and subjected to a new interpretation.

The events surrounding the resignation from the rectorship may have also prompted Heidegger to alter the title of the lecture at short notice. In the course catalogue of the summer semester of 1934, the lecture is announced under the title "The State and Science" (Tues., Thurs., 5:00–6:00 p.m.). According to reports of several students, Heidegger announced the alteration at the beginning of the first lecture lesson categorically and demonstratively with the words "I am teaching *Logic*"—to the surprise and disgruntlement of several NS-functionaries who had turned up to his lecture.

The Heideggerean manuscript of this lecture must be considered lost at present. In all probability, it was lent out by Heidegger and then never returned. In spite of several want ads by the executor of the estate, Dr. Hermann Heidegger, so far no reaction has been received from the present owner. Martin Heidegger himself mentions in a letter from April of 1954 that he wants "soon" to "deal with" the lecture from the summer semester of 1934 with his brother. Accordingly, at this point in time the manuscript must still have existed. Since then, however, the trace disappears.

For the edition, four or rather five documents were available to me:

1. One transcript handwritten in German script by Dr. Wilhelm Hallwachs—written down on both sides of his invoice forms "District Medical Officer, Dr. Hallwachs." It is the most detailed document. The last two of Heidegger's lecture hours (in the present version from §28a onwards) are, according to the statement made by Hallwachs, an exact copy of the Heideggerean lecture manuscript.

2. One transcript by Siegfried Bröse—likewise handwritten in German script. This transcript no longer follows Heidegger's *ductus* exactly, but is an abridgement and revision of that which was presented by Heidegger. It was used above all when the transcript by Hallwachs had gaps or rather was unintelligible—and was then also very helpful.

3. A typescript composed by Helmut Ibach in August and September of 1934, which resulted from a revision of the transcript by Luise Grosse. The typescript came from the estate of Alois Schuh, and is the property of the library of the Philosophical-Theological University St. Georgen in Frankfurt a. M. The copy that was on hand for me is a gift by Dr. Christoph von Wolzogen, to whom warm thanks are due for this from all those interested in Heidegger's thinking. The typescript is abridged a second time compared to Bröse's transcript. However, it was, nevertheless, occasionally referred to for a better understanding of the transcript by Hallwachs. Here too, the last lecture hours were copied from Heidegger's manuscript, with only small deviations compared to Hallwachs'.

4. The volume published by Victor Farías "Lógica. Lecciones de M. Heidegger (semestre verano 1934) en el legado de Helene Weiss"—a, as can be read here, "transcript of an unknown woman, copied from it incompletely." (According to the state of

affairs, the "unknown woman" can have been none other than Luise Grosse.) Apart from the fact that with this pirate edition Farías has violated the copyright, not a word is to be wasted on this publication—or perhaps, after all, one: If one reads the passages that Farías placed as motto in front of his publication, in the context with the lecture as it is in hand with this volume 38, one thus obtains nothing short of a textbook example of how one may *not* cite. One experiences much of Farías' unmistakably tendentious intention, absolutely nothing of Heidegger's train of thought. It is thus also true here: *Nullus est liber tam malus, ut non aliqua parte prosit.*

5. After the completion of the print typescript, I received the copy of a typed transcript, which the Deutsche Literaturarchiv (Marbach a. N.) had acquired shortly before from the estate of Luise Krohn, née Grosse. It concerns the typewritten copy of the transcript of the lecture by Luise Grosse (later: married Krohn), which has been the basis for the revision by Helmut Ibach (cf. above). A comparison with the previously mentioned transcripts indicates that this typed copy contains no usable textual-overruns or textual-variations, which would have to be worked into the version presented here.

For the collation and review of this edition, my sincere thanks are addressed to Dr. Hermann Heidegger, Prof. Dr. Friedrich-Wilhelm von Herrmann and Dr. Hartmut Tietjen. To the latter, I am also indebted for numerous comments concerning the arrangement of the manuscript. I know myself to be cordially indebted to Mr. Ralf Jochen Ehresmann for the transfer of the Hallwachs-manuscript to electronic data carriers, to Ms. Ulrike Ordon for valuable suggestions for the production of the print typescript. I thank finally Ms. Susanne Weiper, M.A. and Mr. Heinrich Gbur for the careful and circumspect proofreading of the printed version.

Bonn, July 1998
Günter Seubold

LEXICON

A

Abyss	*Abgrund*
Actual	*wirklich*
Actuality	*Wirklichkeit*
After the manner of decision	*entscheidungsmäßig*
Ahistoricality	*Geschichtslosigkeit*
Alienated	*entfremdet*
Alienation	*Entfremdung*
Ambiguity	*Vieldeutigkeit, Zweideutigkeit*
Ambiguous	*vieldeutig, zweideutig*
Analysis	*Auseinanderlegung, Zerlegung*
Animal-like being	*tierhaftes Sein*
Announce, to	*ankündigen*
Answering	*Antworten*
Answering for	*Verantworten*
Appropriate, to	*aneignen*
Area of being	*Seinsgebiet*
Area of objects	*Gegenstandsgebiet*
Ascertainability	*Feststellbarkeit*
Ascertainable	*festellbar*
Ask, to	*fragen [verlohnen]*
Assembly	*Zusammenbau*
Atemporal	*Zeitlos*
Atemporality	*Zeitlosigkeit*
Attend toward, to	*entgegenwarten*
Attitude of knowing	*Wissenshaltung*
Attitude	*Stellungnahme*
Attune, to	*stimmen*

Attuned-through	*durchstimmt*
Attunement	*Gestimmtheit*
Awakening	*Erweckung*

B

Battle	*Kampf*
Bearing	*Haltung*
Becomeness	*Gewordenheit*
Becoming	*Werden*
Becoming-character	*Werdecharakter*
Becoming-other	*Anderswerden*
Been, the	*Gewesene, das*
Beenness	*Gewesenheit*
Behavior	*Benehmen*
Being	*Sein, das*
Being-able-to-know	*Wissenkönnen, wissenkönnen*
Being-attuned	*Gestimmtsein*
Being-attuned-through	*Durchstimmtsein*
Being-born-by	*Getragensein*
Being-carried-forward	*Nach-vorne-getragen-sein*
Being-completed	*Abgeschlossensein*
Being-determined	*Bestimmtsein*
Being-elated	*Beflügeltsein*
Being-elevated	*Erhobensein*
Being-exposed	*Ausgesetztsein*
Being-for-one-another	*Füreinandersein*
Being-historical	*Geschichtlichsein, seinsgeschichtliches*
Being-human	*Menschsein*
Being-I	*Ichsein*
Being-in-time	*In-der-Zeit-Sein*
Being-involved	*Eingelassensein*
Being-moved	*Bewegtsein*
Being-object	*Gegenstandsein*
Being-possible	*Seinkönnen*
Being-present-at-hand	*Vorhandensein*
Being-repressed	*Niedergehaltensein*
Beings	*Seiende, das*
Being-subject	*Subjektsein*
Being-temporal	*Zeitlich-Sein, Zeitlichsein*
Being-thing	*Dingsein*
Being-thrown-ahead	*Vorausgeworfensein*
Being-transported	*Entrücktsein*
Being-underway	*Unterwegsein*
Being-with	*Mitsein*

Being-with-one-another	*Miteinandersein*
Belongingness	*Zugehörigkeit, Zusammengehörigkeit*
Bidding	*Geheiß*
Blasting	*Sprengung*
Blasting open	*Aufsprengung*
Bloodline	*blutmäßige, Erbblut, Geblüt*
Body	*Körper, Leib*
Boredom	*Langeweile*

C

Capability	*Fähigkeit*
Capability of being asked	*Fragbarkeit*
Capable of existence	*daseinsfähig*
Captious	*verfänglich*
Captiousness	*Verfänglichkeit*
Care	*Sorge*
Causal connections	*Kausalzusammenhänge*
Cause	*Ursache*
Cause-connection	*Ursachenzusammenhang*
Center	*Mitte*
Character	*Charakter*
Character of concept	*Begriffscharakter*
Character of decision	*Entscheidungscharakter*
Character of history	*Geschichtscharakter*
Citizenship	*Staatsangehörigkeit*
Co-determinant	*mitbestimmendes*
Co-determined	*mitbestimmt, mit bestimmt*
Co-determining	*mitbestimmend*
Cognizance	*Kenntnisnahme*
Coming into being, the	*Entstehen, das*
Coming to nothing, the	*Zunichtewerden, das*
Coming up, the	*Heraufkommen, das*
Commonness	*Geläufigkeit*
Communication	*Mitteilung, Verständigung*
Community	*Gemeinschaft*
Completion	*Abgeschlossenheit*
Comportment	*Verhalten*
Comprehend, to	*begreifen*
Concealed	*verborgen*
Concealedness	*Verborgenheit*
Concept	*Begriff*
Concept of truth	*Wahrheitsbegriff*
Conception	*Auffassung*
Conception of the world	*Weltauffassung*

Conceptual mistake	*Mißgriff*
Conceptuality	*Begrifflichkeit*
Conduct	*Gehabe*
Confrontation	*Auseinandersetzung*
Connections of development	*Enwicklungszusammenhänge*
Consciousness	*Bewußtsein*
Consequence	*Folge*
Consideration	*Betrachtung*
Constancy	*Beständigkeit*
Constant	*beständige, ständige*
Contingencies	*Zufälle, Zufälligkeiten*
Corporeality	*Leiblichkeit*
Correct	*richtig, Richtiges*
Counter-appearance	*Gegenerscheinung*
Counter-concept	*Gegenbegriff*
Counter-meaning	*Gegenbedeutung*
Counter-representation	*Gegenvorstellung*
Course	*Verlauf*
Course of (the/a) question	*Fragerichtung*
Creational	*schaffend*
Crossing	*Übergang*

D

Dasein	*Dasein*
Decaying, the	*das Verwesen*
Decision	*Entscheidung*
Decision-like	*entscheidungshaft*
Decisiveness	*Entschiedentheit*
Decline	*Untergang*
Decree	*Fügung*
Deliberate	*willentlich*
Delimitation	*Umgrenzung*
Delivered over	*überantwortet*
Delivery over	*Überantwortung*
Depending-on-oneself	*Auf-sich-selbst-Stellen*
De-ranged	*ver-rückt*
Descent	*Abstammung*
Destiny	*Schicksal*
Determinateness	*Bestimmtheit*
Determination	*Bestimmung*
Determination of the beginning	*Anfangsbestimmung*
Determination of the essence	*Wesensbestimmung*
Determine, to	*bestimmen*
Dialogue	*Gespräch*

Difference	*Unterschied*
Disavowal	*Verleugnung*
Discipline	*Disziplin, Zucht*
Disclose, to	*eröffnen*
Discourse	*Rede*
Discourse-complex	*Redezusammenhang*
Disposing over	*Verfügung*
Distinctive	*ausgezeichnet*
Drive to live	*Lebensdrang*
Duration	*Dauer*

E

Effective	*wirksam*
Egoism	*Ichsucht, Eigensucht, Egoismus*
Egoist	*ichsüchtiges*
Elapse, to	*verlaufen*
Element of determination	*Bestimmungsstück*
Empowering	*Ermächtigung*
Emptiness	*Leere*
Emptying	*Entleerung*
Encapsulatedness	*Abgekapseltheit*
Endure, to	*ausdauern*
Engaged	*eingerückt*
Engagedness	*Eingerücktheit*
Enigmatic	*rätselhaft*
Ensnared	*befangen*
Ensnarement	*Befangenheit*
Entangled	*befangen, verfallen, verwickelt*
Entering into	*Eintreten*
Entrust, to	*überantworten*
Era	*Zeitalter*
Essence	*Wesen*
Essence, to	*wesen*
Essencing	*Wesung*
Essential ground	*Wesensgrund*
Essential-jointure	*Wesensgefüge*
Event	*Ereignis, Geschehnis*
Experience	*Erfahrung, [Erlebnis]*
Experience-like	*Erlebnishaftes*
Experiences	*Kenntnisse, [Erlebnisse]*
Explorable	*erkundbar*
Explored	*erkundet*
Exploring	*Erkunden*
Exposed	*ausgesetzt*

Exposedness	*Aussgesetztheit*
Expression	*Ausdruck*
Expropriation	*Enteignung*
Extant	*vorfindlich, vorliegen*
Extending	*Erstreckung*

F

Fact	*Tatsache*
Factual content	*Sachhaltigkeit*
Factuality	*Sachgemäßheit*
Factually	*faktisch*
Falling into	*verfallen*
Fatality, the	*Fatale, das*
Fate	*Geschick/Schickung*
Fitted	*eingefügt*
Flight	*Flucht*
Flow/ to flow	*Ablauf, ablaufen*
Flowing off	*Abfließen*
Fore-conception	*Vorausfassung*
Fore-conceptual	*vorbegrifflich*
Fore-decision	*Vorentscheidung*
Fore-field	*Vorfeld*
Fore-grasp, to	*vorgreifen*
Fore-grasping	*vorgreifendes*
Fore-question	*Vorfrage*
Fore-questioning	*Vorfragen*
Forespoken	*vorausgesprochen*
Fore-thrust	*Vorstoß*
Fore-thrusting	*vorstoßen*
Fore-understanding	*Vorverständnis*
Fore-view	*Vorblick*
For-one-another, the	*Füreinander, das*
Forthcoming	*künftig*
Foundation	*Fundament, Grundlage*
Fountain	*Quelltrunk*
Framework	*Rahmen*
Fullness	*Fülle*
Fundamental bearing	*Grundhaltung*
Fundamental constitution	*Grundverfassung*
Fundamental determinations	*Grundbestimmungen*
Fundamental events	*Grundgeschehnisse*
Fundamental experience	*Grunderfahrung*
Fundamental forms	*Grundformen*
Fundamental moods	*Grundstimmungen*

Fundamental phenomenon	*Grunderscheinung*
Fundamental piece	*Grundstück*
Fundamental position	*Grundstellung*
Fundamental power	*Grundmacht*
Fundamental question	*Grundfrage*
Fundamental rule	*Grundregel*
Fundamental structures	*Grundgebilde*
Fundamental task	*Grundaufgabe*
Fundamental word	*Grundwort*
Fundamentally	*grundsätzlich, im Grunde*
Further-question	*Weiterfrage*
Futural	*zukünftig*
Futurality	*Zukünftigkeit*
Futurally	*zukünftig*
Futurally-has been	*zukünftig-gewesenes*

G

Generation	*Geschlecht*
Genuine	*echt*
Gliding away	*weggleiten*
Gliding-away, the	*Weggleiten, das*
Going into	*Eingehen*
Great, the	*Große, das*
Guiding principle	*Leitsatz*
Guiding question	*Leitfrage*

H

Hackneyed truth	*Allerweltswahrheit*
Happening of education	*Erziehungsgeschehen*
Happening, the	*Geschehen, das*
Having-become	*Gewordensein*
Heralding	*Künderschaft*
Hereditary blood connection	*Erbblutzusammenhang*
Heredity	*Vererbung*
Historical being	*geschichtliches Sein*
Historicity	*Geschichtlichkeit*
Historiography	*Historie*
History	*Geschichte*
How-question	*Wiefrage*
Human being	*menschliche Sein*
Human being, the	*Mensch, der*

I

I, the	*das Ich*
Idea	*Darstellung, Vorstellung*
Idle talk	*Gerede*
I-emphasis	*Ich-Betonung*
I-likeness	*Ichhaftigkeit*
Illusion	*Erdichtung*
I-Myself	*Ich-Selbst*
In the midst of	*inmitten*
Incident	*Begebenheit, Vorfall*
Inclusiveness	*Einbezogenheit*
Individualized	*vereinzelt*
Individuation	*Vereinzelung*
Indolence	*Faulheit*
I-ness	*Ichheit*
Inevitability	*Unumgänglichkeit*
In-one-another, the	*Ineinander, das*
Inquired, the	*Befragten, die*
Insistence	*Inständigkeit*
Interwovenness	*Verwobenheit*
In-timely	*Innerzeitig*
I-originated	*Ichentsprungenes*
I-related	*Ichbezogenes*
Irresoluteness	*Unentschlossenheit*
I-time	*Ich-Zeit*

J

Joint	*Fuge*
Joint-execution	*Mitvollzug*
Jointure	*Gefüge*
Judgment	*Beurteilung, Urteil*

K

Keep open, to	*offenhalten*
Keep up, to	*durchhalten*
Kind	*Art*
Kind of being	*Art des Seins, Seinsart*
Kind of essence	*Wesensart*
Knowing, the	*Wissen, das*
Knowing/ that knows	*wissend*

L

Labor	*Arbeit*
Labor, to	*arbeiten*

Language	*Sprache*
Launching of the question	*Frageansatz*
Launching	*Ansatz*
Leading-back-again	*Wiederrückführung*
Leap	*Sprung, Springen*
Liberation	*Befreiung*
Likeness	*Gleichheit*
Line of sight	*Blickrichtung*
Lineage	*Geschlecht*
Linguistics	*Sprachwissenschaft*
Listening-together	*Mithören*
Living being	*Lebewesen*
Lockedness	*Verschlossenheit*
Logic	*Logik*
Lore	*Kunde*
Lore of history	*Geschichtskunde*

M

Making-presence	*Anwesendmachen*
Making-present	*Gegenwärtigung*
Mandate	*Auftrag*
Manifested	*bekundet*
Manifestness	*Offenbarkeit*
Manifoldness	*Mannigfaltigkeit*
Material content	*Sachgehalt*
Matter	*Sache*
Meaning	*Bedeutung*
Mental	*geistliches*
Mental faculties	*Seelenvermögen*
Mis-questioning	*Fehlfragen*
Mission	*Sendung*
Moment	*Augenblick*
Movement	*Bewegung*
Moving, the	*Bewegendes, das*
Mystery	*Geheimnis*

N

Nature-happening	*Naturgeschehen*
Necessity	*Notwendigkeit*
Need	*Not*
No-more, a	*Nichtmehr, ein*
Nonbeing	*Nichtsein*
Non-conceptual	*unbegrifflich*
Non-essence	*Nichtwesen*

Nothing, the	*Nichts, das*
Not-I, the	*Nicht-Ich, das*
Not-yet, a	*Noch-nicht, ein*
Now, the	*Jetzt, das*
Nugatory	*Verneinend*

O

Object	*Gegenstand*
Ob-ject	*Gegen-stand*
Objectifiable	*gegenstandsfähig*
Objectification	*Objektivierung, Vergegenständlichung*
Objective	*vergegendständlicht*
Objectivity	*Objektivität*
Occurrence	*Vorkommen*
Open, the	*Freie, das*
Opened	*aufgeschlossen*
Order	*Ordnung*
Orientation	*Ausrichtung*
Origin	*Herkunft, Ursprung*
Original	*ursprünglich*
Original beginning	*Uranfang*
Original opposition	*Urgegensatz*
Originality	*Ursprünglichkeit*
Overcoming	*Überkommen, Überwindung*

P

Pass, to (as in passing a test)	*bestehen*
Passing of time	*Zeitverlauf*
Passing-by-questioning	*Vorbeifragen*
Past	*Vergangenheit*
Peculiarity	*Sonderheit*
Philosophy	*Philosophie*
Place, a	*Statt, eine*
Poetry	*Dichtung*
Pointing out	*Aufzeigen*
Power	*Kraft, Macht*
Power-jointure	*Machtgefüge*
Precede, to	*vorausgehen*
Predetermined	*vorbestimmt*
Preeminence	*Vorrang*
Preform	*Vorform*
Pregiven	*vorgegeben*
Prejudice	*Vorurteil, Vormeinung*
Presence	*Anwesenheit*

Present, the	*Gegenwart, die*
Present-at-hand	*Vorhanden*
Presentness	*Gegenwärtigkeit*
Preservation	*Bewahrung*
Preserving	*Aufbewahren, bewahrend*
Presupposition	*Voraussetzung*
Primal-event	*Urgeschehnis*
Process	*Verfahren, Vorgang*
Pronounce, to	*aussprechen*
Pronounced	*aussgesprochen*
Pronounced before	*vorgesprochen*
Proper	*eigentlich*
Proposition	*Aussage*
Propositional	*aussagendes*
Pseudo-unity	*Scheineinheit*
Psychical	*seelisch*

Q

Quality	*Eigenschaft*
Question connection	*Fragezusammenhang*
Question form	*Frageform*
Question forth, to	*hervorfragen*
Question of decision	*Entscheidungsfrage*
Question of the essence	*Wesensfrage*
Question realm	*Fragebereich*
Question step	*Frageschritt*
Question wrongly, to	*fehlfragen*
Questionability	*Fraglichkeit*
Questionable	*fragbar, fraglich*
Question-away, to	*wegfragen*
Questioning	*Fragen*
Questioning-concerning-us-ourselves	*Nach-uns-selbst-Fragen*
Questionless	*fraglos*
Questionlessness	*Fraglosigkeit*
Question-strong	*fragekräftig*

R

Race	*Rasse*
Racial	*Rassisches*
Racial movement	*völkische Bewegung*
Reaching over	*Übergriff, das; Übergreifen, das*
Read off, to	*ablesen*
Readiness	*Bereitschaft*
Realm	*Bereich*

Realm of being	*Seinsbereich*
Reason	*Vernunft*
Reeducation	*Umerziehung*
Reference	*Bezug*
Reflection	*Besinnung*
Reflectiveness	*Reflektiertheit*
Reflexion	*Reflexion*
Reflexivity	*Rückbezüglichkeit*
Reforming	*Umprägung*
Region	*Bezirk*
Regulation	*Regelsetzung, Regelung*
Relation	*Beziehung*
Relationship	*Verhältnis*
Remain, to	*bleiben, verbleiben*
Remaining, a	*Verbleib, ein*
Repeated	*nachgesprochen*
Replied to	*beantwortet*
Replying	*Entgegnen*
Representation	*Darstellung, Vorstellung*
Resoluteness	*Entschlossenheit*
Resolution	*Entschluß*
Responsibility	*Verantwortung*
Restlessness	*Unruhe*
Retaining	*Behalten*
Retreat	*Rückzug*
Retrogression	*Rückgang*
Reverence	*Ehrfurcht*
Reversal	*Verkehrung*
Revolution	*Revolution; Umwälzung*

S

Sacrifice	*Opfer*
Say, to	*sagen*
Saying	*Sagen, das*
Science	*Wissenschaft*
Science of history	*Geschichtswissenschaft*
Secondary ranking	*Zweitrangigkeit*
Self	*Selbst*
Self-affirmation	*Selbstbehaupten*
Self-being	*Selbstsein*
Self-centeredness	*Ichbezogenheit*
Self-character	*Selbstcharakter*
Self-conception	*Selbstauffassung*
Self-*Dasein*	*Selbst-Dasein*

Self-deciding	*Selbstentscheiden*
Self-decision	*Selbstentscheidung*
Self-determination	*Selbstbestimmung*
Self-forgottenness	*Selbstvergessenheit*
Self-forlornness	*Selbstverlorenheit*
Selfhood	*Selbstheit*
Selfishness	*Eigensucht, Selbstsucht*
Self-locking	*sich verschließende*
Self-moving	*Selbstbewegen*
Self-opening	*Sichöffnen*
Self-sameness	*Selbigkeit*
Semblance	*Anschein, Schein*
Sense	*Sinn*
Sense of time	*Zeitsinn*
Sense, to	*spüren*
Sequence of the question	*Fragefolge*
Setting-away	*Wegstellen*
Severity	*Härte, Strenge*
Shake up, to	*erschüttern*
Shaking up	*Erschütterung*
Showing	*Aufweisen*
Singularity	*Einmaligkeit*
Site of origin	*Ursprungsort*
Snapping	*Schnappen*
Snazzy	*rassiges*
Society	*Gesellschaft*
Soil	*Boden, Erdboden*
Solitude	*Einsamkeit*
Somewhere to stay	*eine Bleibe*
Soul	*Seele*
Space	*Raum*
Speak along, to	*mitreden*
Speak together, to	*mitsprechen*
Speak, to	*sprechen*
Speaking	*Sprechen, das*
Spirit	*Geist*
Spiritual	*geistliches*
Standard	*maßgebend*
Standardization	*Normung*
Standing	*Stehen*
Standing opposite	*entgegenstehend, gegenüberstehendes*
Standing-opposite	*Gegenüberstehen*
Standing-out	*Ausstehen*
Standing-through	*Durchstehen*

Standpoint	*Standpunkt*
State of affairs	*Tatbestand*
State, the	*Staat, der*
Statement	*Satz, Feststellung*
Staying	*Bleiben*
Stepping away	*Wegsteigende*
Strangeness	*Befremdlichkeit*
Structure	*Bau, Gebilde, Gefüge*
Subject	*Subjekt*
Subject-character	*Subjektcharakter*
Subjectified	*subjektiviert*
Subjectifying	*Subjektivierung*
Subjectivity	*Subjektivität*
Subsist, to	*bestehen*
Subsistence	*Bestand, Bestehen*

T

Take over, to	*Übernehmen*
Taking direction	*Einschlagerichtung, Einschlagsrichtung*
Taking in, a	*Hineinnehmen, ein*
Talk, to	*reden*
Talking	*Reden, das*
Task	*Aufgabe*
Temporality	*Zeitlichkeit*
Temporalize, to	*zeitigen*
Temporalizing	*Zeitigung*
That which belongs to the I	*das dem Ich Zugehörige*
That which dates back	*Zurückliegende, das*
That which disappears	*Verschwindende, das*
That which essences	*wesende; Wesende, das*
That which essences from earlier on	*von früher Wesende, das*
That which goes by	*Vergehen, das*
That which has become	*Gewordene, das*
That which has been	*Gewesene, das*
That which has come to conclusion	*zum Abschluß Gekommene, das*
That which has strayed hither	*Herzugelaufene, das*
That which is	*Seiende, das*
That which is anecdote-like	*Anekdotenhafte, das*
That which is asked about	*Befragte, das*
That which is bygone	*Vergangene, das*
That which is completed	*Abgeschlossene, das*
That which is decisive	*Entscheidende, das*
That which is distinctive	*Auszeichnende, das*
That which is earlier	*Ehemalige, das; Frühere, das*

That which is effective	*Wirksame, das*
That which is essential	*Wesentliche, das*
That which is everyday	*Alltägliche, das*
That which is excessive	*Übermäßige, das*
That which is extant	*Vorliegendes, das*
That which is extraordinary	*Außerordentliche, das*
That which is finished	*Fertige, das*
That which is fixed	*Festliegende, das*
That which is forthcoming	*Künftige, das*
That which is futural	*Zukünftige, das*
That which is handed down	*Überkommene, das*
That which is hostile	*Feindliche, das*
That which is I-like	*Ichhafte, das*
That which is inevitable	*Unumgängliche, das; Zwangsläufige, das*
That which is insignificant	*Belanglose, das*
That which is I-originated	*Ichentsprungene, das*
That which is I-related	*Ichbezogen, das*
That which is news-like	*Nachrichtenmäßige, das*
That which is no more	*das nicht mehr Seiende*
That which is of secondary rank	*Zweitrangige, das*
That which is of the present	*Gegenwärtige, das*
That which is of today	*Heutige, das*
That which is overpowering	*Übermächtige, das*
That which is persevering	*Beharrliche, das*
That which is questioned	*Gefragte, das*
That which is racy	*Rassige, das*
That which is reckonable	*Berechenbare, das*
That which is represented	*Vorgestellte, das*
That which is said	*Gesagte, das*
That which is strange	*Befremdliche, das*
That which is temporal	*Zeitliche, das*
That which is thing-like	*Dinghafte, das*
That which is transient	*Vergängliche, das*
That which is uncreated	*Ungeschaffene, das*
That which is unhistorical	*Ungeschichtliche, das*
That which is unreckonable	*Unberechenbare, das*
That which is unusual	*ungewöhnliche*
That which is usual	*Herkömmliche, das*
That which lies back	*Zurückliegende, das*
That which lies opposite	*Entgegenliegende, das*
That which once was	*Ehemalige, das; Ehemals, das*
That which perseveres	*Beharrliche, das*
That which remains	*Bleibende, das*
That which stands opposite	*Entgegenstehende, das*

That which strayed-hither	*Herzugelaufene, das*
Thing	*Ding*
Thinking	*Denken*
Time	*Zeit*
Time-analysis	*Zeitanalyse*
Time-character	*Zeitcharakter*
Time-concept	*Zeitbegriff*
Time-conception	*Zeitauffassung*
Time-determination	*Zeitbestimmung*
Time-duration	*Zeitdauer*
Time-flow	*Zeitablauf*
Time-formation	*Zeitbildung*
Timely	*Zeitgemäß*
Time-powers	*Zeitmächte*
Time-realm	*Zeitbereich*
Time-relationship	*Zeitverhältnis*
Time-span	*Zeitspanne*
Tradition	*Überlieferung*
Transferal	*Übereignung*
Transferred	*übereignet*
Transformation	*Umwandlung, Wandlung*
Transience	*Vergänglichkeit*
Transported	*entrückt*
Transportedness	*Entrücktheit*
Transporting	*Entrückung*
Transposed	*versetzt*
True	*wahr*
Truth	*Wahrheit*
Turn around, to	*umwenden*
Turn back again, to	*zurückwenden*
Turning around	*Umkehrung*
Turning away	*Abkehr*
Turning back	*Rückwendung*

U

Uncanniness	*Unheimlichkeit*
Uncanny	*unheimlich*
Unconcealedness	*Unverborgenheit*
Unessence	*Unwesen*
Unessential	*unwesentlich*
Unhistorical	*ungeschichtlich*
Unhistoricity	*Ungeschichtlichkeit*
Unhistory	*Ungeschichte*
Unison	*Einklang*

Unpower	*Unmacht*
Unrest	*Unruhe*
Untouchability	*Unberührbarkeit*
Untrue	*Unwahr*
Untruth	*Unwahrheit*
Unveil, to	*enthüllen*
Uprooting	*Entwurzelung*

V

Veil, to	*verhüllen*
Veiled	*verhülltes*
Veiling	*Verschleierung*
Violence	*Gewaltsamkeit*
Volk/Völker	*Volk/Völker*

W

Weltanschauung/Weltanschauungen	*Weltanschauung/Weltanschauungen*
We-ourselves	*Wir-Selbst*
We-time	*Wir-Zeit*
What is asked about	*Gefragte, das*
What-being	*Wassein*
What-concept	*Wasbegriff*
What-determination	*Wasbestimmung*
What-question	*Wasfrage*
Who-question	*Werfrage*
Will of rule	*Herrschaftswille*
Within-timely	*innerzeitig*
Within-timeness	*Innerzeitigkeit*
With-one-another	*Miteinander, Ineinander*
Without history	*geschichtslos*
Word	*Wort*
Word-determination	*Wortbestimmung*
Words	*Wörter*
Word-world	*Wortwelt*
Work, the	*Gemächte, das*
Work, to	*werken*
World	*Welt*
World-conception	*Weltauffassung*
World-forming	*weltbildend*
World-happening	*Weltgeschehen*
World-position	*Weltstellung*
Worthiness of question	*Fragwürdigkeit*
Worthy of question	*fragwürdig*

NOTES

1. See Silvio Vietta, "Wandel unseres Daseins: Eine unbekannte Vorlesung Martin Heideggers von 1934." In: *Frankfurter Allgemeine Zeitung* (18.10.2006), Nr. 242, Beilage "Geisteswissenschaften," N3.
2. Martin Heidegger, *Unterwegs zur Sprache* (Pfullingen: Neske, 1959; 7th ed., 1982), 93; translated as *On the Way to Language*, trans. Peter D. Hertz (New York: Harper & Row, 1971), 8.
3. Martin Heidegger, *Was Heisst Denken?* (Tübingen: Niemeyer, 1984), 100; translated as *What is Called Thinking?*, trans. J. Glenn Gray (New York: Harper and Row, 1968), 154.